DO' WITH THE LAW

Anarchist Individualist Writings from
Early Twentieth-Century France

Edited by Mitchell Abidor

AK Press
Chico | Edinburgh

*Down with the Law: Anarchist Individualist Writings from
Early Twentieth-Century France*
© 2019 Mitchell Abidor

ISBN: 978–1-84935–344–1
E-ISBN: 978–1-84935–345–8
Library of Congress Control Number: 2019933776

AK Press
370 Ryan Ave. #100
Chico, CA 95973
www.akpress.org
akpress@akpress.org

AK Press
33 Tower St.
Edinburgh EH6 7BN
Scotland
www.akuk.com
ak@akedin.demon.co.uk

The above addresses would be delighted to provide you with the latest AK
Press distribution catalog, which features books, pamphlets, zines, and stylish
apparel published and/or distributed by AK Press. Alternatively, visit our web-
sites for the complete catalog, latest news, and secure ordering.

Cover and interior design by Margaret Killjoy

Cover illustration by Flavio Costantini, *Les Travailleurs de la nuit I. Parigi, 1
ottobre 1901*, 1964. Courtesy Archivio Flavio Costantini, Genova

CONTENTS

Introduction 1

Albert Libertad. 9
The Carrion Cult 12
To the Resigned 18
Down with the Law! 21
Fear 24
Spineless Meat 27

Émile Armand. 29
Is the Anarchist Ideal Realizable?. 31
Principal Tendencies and Theses of the "Unique" Center . . .33
On Sexual Freedom 34
What Is an Anarchist? 36
Is the Illegalist Anarchist Our Comrade? 40

Marius Jacob 51
Why I Stole 53

André Lorulot. 59
Who Are We? What Do We Want?. 61
Men Digust Me 67

Han Ryner 75
Antipatriotism *76*
Mini-Manual of Individualism. *79*

Georges Palante 123
Individualism *124*
The Relationship between Pessimism and Individualism . .*126*
The Future of Pessimism and Individualism *131*

Victor Serge 133
The Communards. *136*
A Head Will Fall *139*

Rirette Maîtrejean 145
Memories of Anarchy *148*

INTRODUCTION

IT IS PERHAPS IRONIC THAT FRANCE, THE COUNTRY OF GREAT MASS revolutions, of 1789, of 1830, of 1848, of the Commune of 1871, of the Popular Front strikes of 1936 and the uprising of May 1968, gave birth to the most diverse and influential group of anarchist individualist thinkers, writers, and militants. Or perhaps it is precisely because of France's revolutionary history that individualism took such firm root. If we examine the country's revolutions and mass movements, what is abundantly clear is that for all its revolutionary fervor, for all the bloodshed and sacrifice, in every case the revolution either served the interests of people other than the workers who made them, or were bloody failures that set the movement back decades.

This failure of the revolutions and mass organizations up to the end of the nineteenth century led to two diametrically opposed reactions among anarchists. On the one hand, there were those who, rather than lose heart and faith in the mass movement, flocked to the revolutionary wing of the Left, particularly syndicalism. For these militants the error was not believing in mass activity, but carrying it out incorrectly. For these people the revolution remained a distinct possibility that would occur in the not-too-distant future. This current included men such as Émile Pouget, editor of *Le Père Peinard*, a newspaper written in popular slang and advocating direct action by the workers, most notably through sabotage. This rebirth of the revolutionary far Left in fin-de-siècle France was the main reason the age of the bomb throwers, of Ravachol, Émile Henry, and August Vaillant, ended so abruptly in 1894: these men had hoped to inspire a mass movement, and once that movement appeared—inspired by them or not—continuing their campaign of terror was unnecessary.

On the other hand, there were those who believed there was no hope for revolution, that the masses, timid, cowed, and uneducated, would never be able to overthrow their masters, or at least not until a long period of education had occurred. Anarchist individualism critiqued the revolutionary illusion, an alternative to the apparently futile attempts to change the world, to the sacrificing of present generations to hypothetical future ones. Anarchist individualists turned things on their head and posited the possibility of liberation today, a liberation within the reach of all at this very moment.

These diametrically opposed positions appealed to equally diametrically opposed types. It has been proposed that the split in the two movements was in large part generational, with older, more "serious" types, such as Kropotkin, Malatesta, the Reclus brothers, and Sébastien Faure supporting a mass-based or at least more "humanist" version of anarchism, while young hotheads such as Albert Libertad, Émile Armand, and André Lorulot favored the more uncompromising individualist trend, one that would cause anarchy within anarchy and that would forever battle on two fronts: against a rotten society they hated and against a worm-ridden anarchist ship too timid to effect any real change. And, as we will see, a third front also existed: a civil war among individualists, one that would result in the virtual disappearance of the movement as a viable force just before World War I.

Anarchist individualism can briefly be summed up as a theory that revolves around the absolute primacy of the individual, and not just that of the abstract individual, but of *my* primacy, of *my* absolute right to define what is good, to refuse any laws and constraints imposed from without, of *my* duty to myself alone. As the scholar Marie-Josephe Dhavernas wrote, "Individualists give the word 'freedom' the sense of the maximum realization by each of his own tendencies and needs, of his own internal laws opposed to the external laws imposed by society." Or as Henri Zisly, an early anarchist individualist, said in the pages of its main organ, *l'anarchie*: "To be an anarchist means absolutely living outside established laws; it's wanting to follow the pure theory, to not work for a boss. It's being completely free of bourgeois prejudices; it's being a supporter of violent methods of social struggle."

Such an idea leaves itself open to the widest variations, from those who, like Victor Serge in "A Head Will Fall," included below, justify killing, to those like Han Ryner, who lays out a gentler, more philosophical version in his "Mini-Manual of Individualism."

What differentiates anarchist individualism from virtually every other revolutionary school is its refusal of textual authority: everyone has a right to develop their own ideas, without the support of any canonical texts. The ferocious Albert Libertad had no use for Ryner's version of anarchism, one inspired by the Stoics and the Cynics, but he could only attack it for what it was, not because it deviated from any line or contradicted an element of the vulgate. The individualists didn't throw different interpretations of their founding father Max Stirner at each other, since quoting anyone, allowing anyone to serve as an authority, constituted an abandonment of the individual's autonomy.

In addition, one will search in vain for anything resembling an economic analysis of reality. Economic forces play no part in anarchist individualism: the individual is either free by his or her own choice or a slave by his or her own choice. Class struggle is simply not part of the equation. How the bourgeoisie assumed power is not an issue that will ever be addressed by individualists because it assumes there is something greater than the individual. If there is any force that restricts the activities of an individual it is the biological: a strict biological determinism was a common

feature of the movement, and only one's biological predisposi-
tions could prevent one from fully being the person one is supposed to be. So, it is not Karl Marx who mattered to them, but
the all-but-forgotten (nonanarchist) biologist Félix Le Dantec.
After all, one of Le Dantec's most important books was titled
*Egoism, the Basis for Every Society: A Study of the Deformations
Resulting from Life in Common.*

Of course, there are philosophers, in particular Max Stirner
and Friedrich Nietzsche, who exerted a tremendous influence
on anarchist individualists of all stripes. These two writers were
just becoming known in France around the turn of the twentieth century, thanks in both cases to the remarkable literary
journal *La Revue Blanche.* Stirner's insistence on the Self, on the
all-importance and total liberty of the individual, can be found
beneath every word written by the individualists, though he is
seldom cited. And not because they were all plagiarists: his ideas
were theirs, and vice versa. In many ways, individualism is more
an attitude than a philosophy, and Stirner's writings were the
first to give that attitude a philosophical basis, one that would be
attacked by Marx in *The German Ideology.*

Nietzsche's case was similar, though some anarchist individualists, particularly Victor Serge as he was beginning to exit
from individualism following his release in 1917 after being
imprisoned for supposedly participating in the depredations of
the Bonnot Gang, saw the dangers in Nietzscheism. Insofar as
Nietzsche sought a transvaluation of all values and insisted on
living a life free of constraints, free of the herd and of slave morality, he was an anarchist individualist *avant la lettre*, and this was
the Nietzsche they admired. They tended to leave to the side the
Nietzsche of the blond beast, the Nietzsche who glorified military
virtues. But again, if we view anarchist individualism as an attitude, Nietzsche was one of them.

Scientific ideas in general, indeed a cult of science, played an
important part in individualist life. It was essential to the individualists to master science and the laws of nature because humanity
itself was a part of nature. Ideas current at the time concerning
overpopulation, the degeneration of the human race, and the

dreadful effects of alcoholism figured prominently in anarchist life. Their fight was a fight against this degeneration, which they viewed as having long-term effects, for to a large extent they were Lamarckians, believers in the heritability of acquired traits. The degraded individuals they saw around them would in their turn produce further generations of degraded beings. As we will see below in Rirette Maîtrejean's account of her time living alongside the members of the Bonnot Gang, it was up to them to begin the process of reviving humanity by rejecting alcohol and coffee, refusing to eat meat, controlling the population, and maintaining physical fitness. So important was the last of these that the murderous members of the Bonnot Gang, when put on trial in 1913 for the crime wave they committed in 1911 and 1912, continued to exercise while in jail, and the evidence against them included barbells alongside rifles and pistols.

* * *

At the heart of anarchist individualism was a profound and barely disguised contempt for the masses, who willingly accept the lot assigned to them. Not only are they the drunks who are a symptom of the ambient degeneracy, they are cowards and spineless. It is no accident that late in his life André Lorulot would write a book-length diatribe, sections of which are included here, called *Men Disgust Me*. In failing to rebel they are complicit in their own enslavement and thus deserve it, for it is only by rebelling that man lives. And the use of the word "man" is not accidental: the highest praise for a person who fights back is that he was "a man." Libertad called those who vote the "electoral cattle," and the masses in general "spineless meat." This view of humanity was perhaps the key reason they dismissed any possibility of revolution.

Their elitism was largely an outgrowth of their own backgrounds: few among them had received educations (Libertad had been raised in a home for abandoned children; Serge was largely an autodidact). If they were able to raise themselves out of the muck, then there was nothing that prevented everyone else from doing the same. Failure to do so was a result not of societal impediments but of personal weakness.

So, for them the enemy was not just the government, it was society itself, which existed only to crush individuality and the individual. This is most clearly found in the writings of Georges Palante, who, while not an anarchist (though his writings did occasionally appear in anarchist journals), was, because of his uncompromising individualism, much admired. His spirit hovers over much of this writing, even when he's not being quoted directly. His profound pessimism was based on the unequal struggle between the individual and the rest of society in which the individual was almost doomed to failure. Palante's unequal struggle with society ended in his suicide.

Not that the individualists didn't hope to change the masses and have them live a new and better life. Because of this, education was an important part of their activity. They did not go to factories to organize unions, which they in any case opposed as yet another element of herd life, nor did they work for electoral candidates, since they opposed voting on principle as a farce (the great Zo d'Axa, founder of the newspaper *L'Endehors*, ran an ass as a candidate in a Parisian election) and expected nothing from the state. But they did have a well-established network of educational groups, most importantly the Causeries Populaires, founded by Libertad in 1902, three years before he founded his newspaper. Talks were given on philosophical subjects, on literature, and on directly anarchist topics, and columns of the anarchist weekly *Les Temps Nouveaux* were filled with announcements for talks being given all over working-class France. When disputes occurred among anarchists, the result was usually the establishing of another study group. Long after Libertad's death in 1908 the Causeries Populaires persisted, with Victor Serge organizing them until his arrest in February 1912, but a dizzying variety of these groups existed throughout France.

Along with talks there were newspapers, most importantly *l'anarchie*, founded by Libertad in 1905 (the title of the paper, all in lowercase letters, was itself a statement, as no letter was more important than another), though the individualists often wrote in other, "enemy" anarchist papers. And just as splits could lead to new study circles, they also led to new newspapers. Included in this anthology is the program of André Lorulot's newspaper *L'Idée Libre*, which spun off from *l'anarchie*, which Lorulot had once edited but left, largely as a result of the controversy over illegalism.

Since anarchist individualism refused to accept any laws or any established morality, illegalism, practicing crime as a political act, was a natural outgrowth of it. Petty crime and grand larceny were significant parts of individualist life, and counterfeiting was a particular favorite. The husband of Rirette Maîtrejean—director of *l'anarchie*, one of the defendants in the Bonnot trial, and Victor Serge's companion—was imprisoned for precisely that. But there was illegalism and there was illegalism.

Marius Jacob was widely admired among the illegalists, and he was easy to admire. Jacob founded a band of criminals called "the Night Workers" who operated all over France from their base in Paris. They tried to avoid physically harming their victims, chose their victims from among the wealthy, and contributed a portion of their takings to the cause. His case for anarchist illegalism, "Why I Robbed," is included here and is a virtual *summum* of illegalist ideas. He represented what we might call the Robin Hood wing of illegalism.

And then there was the Bonnot Gang. This group of anarchists, many of whom had known each other as youths in Brussels and who met up in Paris in the offices of *l'anarchie*, were led by a figure less directly tied to established anarchist circles, Jules Bonnot. Unlike Jacob, they had no compunction about killing and did so whenever they felt threatened. During their crime wave in 1911 and 1912 they stole cars, robbed banks, and shot down police officers and simple employees, all of whom they regarded as the enemy. They were the reductio ad absurdum of anarchist individualism, men who took its tenets to their furthest degree, and the debates over their tactics were long and stormy. Émile Armand wrote about them in his article "Is the Illegalist Anarchist Our Comrade?," and Victor Serge, editor during the crime wave, was arrested and tried in part for his role as theoretician of illegalism.

The Bonnot Affair ended with some gang members killed in shootouts with the police, others executed, yet others sent to prison (including Serge, who was not actually part of the gang), and the virtual death of anarchist individualism as a movement of any importance. Illegalism had laid bare all the flaws inherent in the movement by acting on its most extreme implications, thus showing it to be a dead end that wasted the lives of its militants.

l'anarchie would fold in 1914, and the fight against World War I would see other, mass schools of anarchism definitively seize the upper hand. Though many of the key figures of the individualist anarchist movement remained active, some for decades, the Bolshevik Revolution and communism drained off much that was revolutionary from the Left. The Bolsheviks showed that a revolution could be successful; though some anarchist individualists, most prominently Armand, rejected the revolution, some had their lives changed permanently by it. Lorulot supported it, as did Victor Serge, who, after being released from prison in 1917 and spending time in Barcelona and then again in a French prison, moved to the Soviet Union, where he became an important propagandist for the revolution. He also expressed the hope that the libertarian ideas he had championed would save the Russian Revolution from falling into tyranny. This utopian hope was probably French anarchist individualism's final failure.

ALBERT LIBERTAD

Libertad is one of those rare figures whose life is actually equal to his legend. Rirette Maîtrejean, who edited his newspaper, l'anarchie, *would later say of him that "he left me my best, my purest memories of anarchy."*

Born Albert Joseph on November 24, 1885, he was abandoned by his parents and brought up in an orphanage in Bordeaux, which he fled while still a teenager. Disabled by a childhood illness, he used crutches to get around. He fled the home while still a teenager and had a reputation as a rebel, which led the police to trail him as a known anarchist from the age of nineteen. According to a police report, on August 27, 1897, he made the inevitable move to Paris where he went to the offices of Sébastien Faure's newspaper, Le Libertaire.

His reputation had been ensured within mere weeks of his arrival in Paris. On September 5, 1897, he attended services at Sacré Coeur, and when the priest launched an attack on anarchists, someone in the crowd shouted: "You're the one causing a scandal and who has unhealthy ideas. You got a lot of damn nerve!"' The crowd fell on Libertad, beating him before turning him over to the police.

The February 26, 1898 issue of Les Temps Nouveaux *tells of right-wing students tearing down a pro-Dreyfus poster and of "comrade Libertad, passing at the same moment, remarking to these individuals that they were in the wrong and that everyone had the right to express his opinion as he saw fit." The crowd attacked Libertad to cries of "Death to the Kikes!" On April 30, 1899, Libertad again stood up to his opponents, this time police officers who were attempting to arrest a comrade, and for this he again was beaten. Libertad, unlike some on the far left, was a fervent supporter of the Dreyfusard cause, and was a collaborator of the Dreyfusard* Journal du Peuple.

His militancy led him to be condemned six times during his ten years in Paris, though, given his reputation, the sentences were quite moderate, none exceeding three months in jail. In one case he was fined a single franc.

Though Libertad was a prolific writer, his official profession was as a proofreader, a favored trade for leftists until well into the twentieth century. He would appear at demonstrations in a printer's smock, waving his crutches, screaming at the police when they would fall on him, "You're hurting me! Don't touch my leg! Don't touch my arm!"

However important his legend as a brawler and battler, Libertad's real influence grew out of his speaking and writing, the former in the "causeries," or talks, that were a staple of anarchist life and the latter in various anarchist journals until he founded his own in 1905.

In 1902 he founded the Causeries Populaires, headquartered in Montmartre at what would later be the offices of l'anarchie, *though the talks were also held at other locales in working-class Paris. At these talks his listeners learned about Stirner and Nietzsche, but the audience also attended talks titled "Anti-Social Labor," "Thinking and Acting," "Anarchist Life," "Rabelais" (whom he had not read), and "Anarchist Ideas."*

Libertad's contempt for society's rules was evident in his private life: he had relationships with the Mahé sisters, Anna and Armandine. He lived with both of them, had romantic relationships with both of them, and founded l'anarchie *with both of them on April 13, 1905. Anna Mahé earned herself a footnote in anarchist history thanks to her attempt—similar to Bernard Shaw's in English—to develop a simplified system of French spelling—for example, "plaizir" instead of "plaisir," "intellijent" instead of "intelligent"—which she used in her published articles.*

l'anarchie *was his principal outlet in his final years, and he died in 1908. According to legend, his death was the result of blows delivered by the police; according to the person who took care of him, he died of anthrax.*

The Carrion Cult

*This pamphlet, published in 1925, is taken from
articles that originally appeared in* l'anarchie. *The
sections in brackets were in the original articles but not
in the pamphlet.*

In a desire for eternal life, men have considered death to be a passage, a painful step, and they have bowed before its "mystery" to the point of venerating it.

Even before men knew how to work with stone, marble, and iron to shelter the living, they knew how to fashion this material to honor the dead.

Churches and cloisters richly immured their tombs beneath their apses and choirs, while huts were huddled against their sides, barely sheltering the living.

The cult of the dead has, from the beginning of time, hindered man's forward march. It is the original sin, the dead weight, the iron ball that humanity drags along behind it.

The voice of death, the voices of the dead has always thundered against the voice of universal life, which is ever-evolving.

Jehovah, who Moses's imagination made burst forth from Sinai, still dictates his laws. Jesus of Nazareth, dead for almost twenty centuries, still preaches his morality. Buddha, Confucius, and Lao Tzu's wisdom still reign. And how many others!

We bear the heavy responsibility of our ancestors; we have their defects and their qualities.

And so, in France we are the children of the Gauls, though we are French via the Francs and are of the Latin race when it comes to the eternal hatred of the Germans. Each of these heredities brings with it obligations.

[We are the oldest children of the church by virtue of who knows which dead, and also the grandchildren of the Great Revolution. We are citizens of the Third Republic and we are also devoted to the Sacred Heart of Jesus. We are born Catholics or Protestants, republicans or royalists, rich or poor. We are always what we are through the dead; we are never ourselves. Our eyes, placed atop our heads, look ahead and, however much they lead us forward, it is always toward the ground where our dead repose, toward the past where the dead lived that our education allows us to guide them.]

Our ancestors ... the past ... the dead. ... Whole peoples have died from this triple respect.

China is exactly where it was thousands of years ago because it has saved the principal place in their homes for their dead.

Death is not only a germ of corruption due to the chemical disintegration of man's body poisoning the atmosphere; it is even more the case through the consecration of the past, the immobilizing of thought at a certain stage of evolution. Living, man's thought would have evolved, would have been more advanced. Dead, it crystallizes. Yet it is this precise moment that the living choose to admire in order to sanctify it, to deify it.

Usages and custom, ancestral errors are communicated from one person to another in the family. People believe in the god of their fathers, in respecting the fatherland of their ancestors. ... Why don't we respect their lighting system, their way of dressing?

Yes, this strange fact occurs that at a time when the envelope, the everyday economy improves, changes, and becomes differentiated; when everything dies and is transformed, that men, the spirit of man, remains in the same state of servitude, mummifies itself in the same errors.

Just as in the century of the torch, in the century of electricity man still believes in the paradises of tomorrow, in the gods of vengeance and forgiveness, in hells and Valhallas as a way of respecting the ideas of his ancestors.

The dead lead us, the dead command us, the dead take the place of the living.

All our festivals, all our glorifications are the anniversaries of deaths and massacres. We celebrate All Saints' Day to glorify the saints of the church, the Feast of the Dead so as not to forget a single dead man. The dead go to Olympus or paradise, to the right hand of Jupiter or God. They fill "immaterial" space and they encumber "material" space with their corteges, their displays, and their cemeteries. If nature didn't take it upon itself to make their bodies disintegrate and to disperse their ashes, the living wouldn't know where to place their feet in the vast necropolis that would be the earth.

The memory of the dead, their acts and deeds, obstruct the brains of children. We only talk to them about the dead, we *should* only speak to them about the dead. We make them live in the realm of the unreal and the past. They must know nothing of the present.

If secularism has dropped the story of Mr. Noah or that of Mr. Moses, it has replaced it with those of Mr. Charlemagne or Mr. Capet. Children know the date of Madame Feregonde's death, but don't have the least notion about hygiene. Some young girls of fifteen know that in Spain a certain Madame Isabelle spent an entire century wearing one blouse but are strangely upset when their first menstrual period comes.

Some women, who have the chronology of the kings of France at the tip of their fingers without a single mistake, don't know what to do with a child who cries for the first time in its life.

Though we leave a young girl next to one who is dying, who is in her final throes, we push her away from a woman whose womb is opening to life.

The dead obstruct cities, streets, and squares. We encounter them in marble, in stone, in bronze. This inscription tells us of their birth, and that plaque tells us where they lived. Squares bear their titles or their exploits. Street names don't indicate their position, form, altitude, or location; they speak of Magenta or Solferino, an exploit of the dead where many were killed. They remind you of Saint Eleuthère or the Chevalier de la Barre, men whose only good quality was that of dying. In economic life it is yet again the dead who plot the lives of all. One sees his entire life darkened by his father's "crime," another wears the halo of the glory, the genius, the daring of his forefathers. This one is born a bumpkin with the most distinguished of minds, that one is born noble with the most vulgar of minds. We are nothing in and of ourselves; we are everything through our ancestors. And yet … in the eyes of scientific criticism, what is death? This respect for the departed, this cult of decrepitude: by what argument can it be justified? Few have asked this, and this is why the question is not resolved.

And in the center of cities, aren't there great spaces that the living piously maintain? These are the cemeteries, the gardens of the dead.

The living think it is a good thing to bury, right next to their children's cradles, piles of decomposing flesh, carrion, the nutritive element of all maladies, the breeding ground of all infections.

They consecrate great spaces planted with magnificent trees in order to deposit typhoid-ridden, pestilential, anthracic bodies there, one or two meters deep. And after a few days the infectious viruses roam the city seeking other victims.

Men who have no respect for their living organism, which they exhaust, which they poison, which they put at risk, are suddenly taken with a comic respect for their mortal remains when they should rid themselves of them as soon as possible, arrange them in the least cumbersome, the most usable form.

The cult of the dead is one of the most vulgar aberrations of the living. It's a holdover from those religions that promised paradise. The dead must be prepared for the visit to the beyond: they must be given weapons so they can participate in the hunts of Veleda, some food for the trip, give them the high viaticum, prepare them to present themselves to God. [Religions depart, but their ridiculous formulas remain. The dead take the place of the living.]

Whole groups of workingmen and workingwomen employ their abilities and energy maintaining the cult of the dead. Men dig up the earth, carve stone and marble, forge fences, prepare a house for them in order to respectfully bury the syphilitic carrion that has just died.

Women weave shrouds, make artificial flowers, fashion bouquets to decorate the house where the decomposing pile of a freshly dead tubercular will repose. Instead of hastening to make these loci of decomposition disappear, of using all the speed and hygiene possible to destroy these evil homes whose preservation and maintenance can only spread death around them, everything possible is done to preserve them as long as possible. These mounds of flesh are paraded around in special wagons, in hearses, through the roads and the streets. When they pass, men remove their hats. They respect the dead.

The amount of effort and matter expended by humanity in maintaining the cult of the dead is unimaginable. If all this energy were used to benefit children thousands and thousands of them would be spared illness and death.

If this imbecilic respect for the dead were to disappear and make room for respect for the living, we would unimaginably increase the health and happiness of human life.

Men accept the hypocrisy of necrophages, of those who eat the dead, of those who live off the dead: from the priest, giver of sacred water, to the merchant of eternal homes; from the wreath seller to the sculptor of mortuary angels. With ridiculous boxes that lead and accompany these grotesque puppets, men proceed to the removal of this human detritus and its distribution in accordance with the state of its fortune, when a good transport service with hermetically sealed cars and a crematory oven constructed in keeping with the latest scientific discoveries would suffice.

[I will not concern myself with the use of ashes, though it would seem to me more worthwhile to employ them as humus rather than carrying them around in little boxes. Men complain about work, yet they don't want to simplify those gestures that overly complicate the occasions of their existence, not even to do away with those for the imbecilic—as well as dangerous—preservation of their cadavers. The anarchists have too much respect for the living to respect the dead. Let us hope that someday this outdated cult will have become a road management service, and that the living will know life in all its manifestations.]

As we've already said, it is because men are ignorant that they surround so simple a phenomenon as death with such religious mumbo jumbo. It also worth noting that this is only the case with human death: the death of other animals and vegetables doesn't serve as the occasion for similar demonstrations. Why?

The first men, barely evolved brutes, devoid of all knowledge, buried the dead man with his living wife, his weapons, his furniture, his jewels. Others had the corpse appear before a tribunal to ask him to give an account of his life. Man has always misunderstood the true meaning of death.

And yet, in nature everything that lives, dies. Every living organism fails when, for one reason or another, the equilibrium between its different functions is broken. The causes of death, the ravages of the illness or the accident that caused the death of the individual, are scientifically determined.

From the human point of view then, there is death, there is disappearance of life, that is, the cessation of a certain activity in a certain form.

But from the general point of view death doesn't exist. There is only life. After what we call death the transformative phenomena continue. Oxygen, hydrogen, gas, and minerals depart in different forms and combine in new ways and contribute to the existence of other living organisms. There is no death; there is a circulation of bodies, modifications in the appearance of matter and energy, endless continuation in time and space of life and universal activity.

A dead man is a body returned to circulation in a triple form: solid, liquid, and gaseous. It is nothing but this, and we should consider and treat it as such.

It is obvious that these positive and scientific concepts leave no room for weepy speculations on the soul, the beyond, the void.

But we know that all those religions that preach the "future life" and the "better world" have the inspiring of resignation among those who are despoiled and exploited.

Rather than kneeling before corpses it would be better to organize life on better foundations in order to derive a maximum amount of joy and well-being from it.

People will be angered by our theories and our disdain: this is pure hypocrisy on their part. The cult of the dead is nothing but an insult to true pain. The fact of maintaining a small garden, of dressing in black, of wearing crepe doesn't prove the sincerity of one's sorrow. This latter must disappear. Individuals must react before the irrevocability and the inevitability of death. We must fight against suffering instead of exhibiting it, parading it in grotesque cavalcades and lying congratulations.

This one, who respectfully follows a hearse, had the day before worked furiously at starving the deceased; that one laments behind a cadaver, but did nothing to come to his assistance when it would have been possible to save his life. Every day capitalist society spreads death by its poor organization, by the poverty it creates, by the lack of hygiene, the deprivation and ignorance from which individuals suffer. By supporting such a society men are the cause of their own suffering, and instead of moaning before destiny they would do better to work at improving their conditions of existence so as to allow human life its greatest development and intensity.

How could we know life when it is only the dead who guide it?

How can we live in the present under the tutelage of the past?

If man wants to live, let him no longer have any respect for the dead, let him abandon the cult of carrion. The dead block the road to progress for the living.

We must tear down the pyramids, the tumuli, the tombs. We must bring the wheelbarrows into the cemeteries so as to rid humanity of what they call respect for the dead, but which is the cult of carrion.

To the Resigned

I hate the resigned!

I hate the resigned, just as I hate the filthy, just as I hate layabouts!

I hate resignation! I hate filthiness, I hate inaction.

I feel for the sick man bent under some malignant fever; I hate the imaginary sick man who would be set on his feet by a little bit of will.

I feel for the man in chains, surrounded by guards, crushed under the weight of irons and the many.

I hate soldiers who bow before weight of braids and three stars; the workers who are bent under the weight of capital.

I love the man who, wherever he is, says what he feels; I hate the believer in voting, perpetually seeking conquest by the majority.

I love the scholar crushed under the weight of scientific research; I hate the individual who bends his body under the weight of an unknown power, of some "X," of a god.

I hate, I say, all those who, surrendering a portion of their strength as men to others through fear or resignation, not only keep their heads down but make me, and those I love, keep our heads down as well through the weight of their frightful collaboration and their idiotic inertia.

I hate them, yes, I hate them, because for my part, I feel all this in my bones. I don't bow before the officer's braid, the mayor's sash, the gold of the capitalist, morality, or religion. For a long time I have known that all of these things are just baubles that we can break like glass. ... I bend beneath the weight of the resignation of others. O how I hate resignation!

I love life.

I want to live, not in a petty way like those who only satisfy some of their muscles, their nerves, but in a grand way, satisfying facial muscles as well as calves, my back as well as my brain.

I don't want to trade a portion of now for a fictive portion of tomorrow. I don't want to surrender anything of the present for the wind of the future.

I don't want to debase anything of myself in the face of the words "fatherland," "God," "honor." I too well know the emptiness of these words, these religious and secular ghosts.

I laugh at pensions, at paradises, the hope for which hope allows religion and capital to maintain a hold on the resigned.

I laugh at those who, saving for their old age, deprive themselves in their youth; those who, in order to eat at sixty, fast at twenty.

I want to eat while I have strong teeth to tear and grind healthy meats and succulent fruits, while my stomach juices digest without a problem I want to drink my fill of refreshing and tonic drinks.

I want to love women, or a woman, depending on our mutual desire, and I don't want to resign myself to the family, to law, to the Penal Code: no one has any rights over our bodies. You want,

I want. Let us laugh at the family, the law, the ancient form of resignation.

But this isn't all. I want, since I have eyes, ears, and other senses, more than just to drink, I want to eat, to enjoy sexual love: to experience joy in other forms. I want to see beautiful sculptures and painting, to admire Rodin and Manet. I want to hear the best opera companies play Beethoven and Wagner. I want to know the classics at the Comédie-Française, to leaf through the literary and artistic baggage left by men of the past to men of the present, or even better, to leaf through the now and forever unfinished oeuvre of humanity.

I want joy for myself, for my chosen companion, for my friends. I want a home where my eyes can agreeably rest when my work is done.

For I want the joy of labor, too, that healthy, that mighty joy. I want my arms to handle the plane, the hammer, the spade, and the scythe; that my muscles develop, the thoracic cage become larger with powerful, useful, and reasoned movements.

I want to be useful; I want us to be useful. I want to be useful to my neighbor and for my neighbor to be useful to me. I desire that we labor much, for I am insatiable for joy. And it is because I want to enjoy myself that I am not resigned.

Yes, yes I want to produce, but I want to enjoy myself. I want to knead the dough, but to eat better bread; to work at the grape harvest, but drink better wine; to build a house, but live in better rooms; make furniture, but possess the useful, see the beautiful; I want to make theaters, but ones big enough to house me and mine.

I want to cooperate in producing, but I also want to cooperate in consuming.

Some dream of producing for others to whom they will leave, oh the irony of it, the best of their efforts. As for me, I want, freely united with others, to produce but also to consume.

You who are resigned, look: I spit on your idols. I spit on God, the Fatherland, I spit on Christ, I spit on the flag, I spit on capital and the golden calf; I spit on laws and Penal Codes, on the symbols of religion; they are baubles, I could care less about them, I laugh at them. …

Only through you do they mean anything; leave them behind and they'll break into pieces.

You are thus a force, you who are resigned, one of those forces that don't know they are one, but who are nevertheless a force, and I can't spit on you, I can only hate you … or love you.

Above all, my desire is to see you shaking off your resignation in a ferocious awakening of life.

There is no future paradise, there is no future; there is only the present.

Let us live!

Live! Resignation is death.

Revolt is life.

[From *l'anarchie*, April 13, 1905.]

Down with the Law!

"The anarchists find M. de La Rochefoucauld and all those who protest without worrying about legality to be logically consistent *with themselves*," Anna Mahé tells us.[1]

This is obviously not correct, as I will demonstrate.

All that is needed is one word to travesty the meaning of a phrase, and so the two words underlined suffice to entirely change the meaning of the one I quote.

If Anna Mahé were the leader of a great newspaper she would hasten to accuse the typographers or the proofreader for the blunder and everything would be for the best in the best of all possible worlds.

Or else she would think it wise to stand by an idea that isn't a manifestation of her reasoning, but rather the act of her pen running away with itself.

---

1   Anna Mahé (1882–1960), individualist and later communist anarchist, Libertad's companion, and campaigner for simplified spelling. She wrote frequently and had editorial responsibilities at *l'anarchie*. —ed.

But on the contrary, she thinks that it is necessary, especially in these lead articles that are viewed as anarchist, to make the fewest errors possible and for us to point them out ourselves when we see them.

It is to me that this falls today.

The Catholics, the socialists, and all those who accept at a given moment the voting system, are not logically consistent with themselves when they rebel against the consequences of a law, when they demonstrate against its agents, its representatives.

Only the anarchists are authorized, are logically consistent *with themselves* when they act against the law.

When a man deposits his ballot in the urn he is not using a means of persuasion that comes from free examination or experience. He is executing the mechanical operation of counting those who are ready to choose the same delegates as he, to consequently make the same laws, to establish the same regulations that all men must submit to. In casting his vote he says: "I trust in chance. The name that will come from this urn will be that of my legislator. I could be on the side of the majority, but I have the chance of being on the side of the minority. Whatever happens, happens."

After coming to an agreement with other men, having decided that they will all defer to the mechanical judgment of number, there is, on the part of those who are the minority when they don't accept the laws and regulations of the majority, a feeling of being fooled, similar to that of a bad gambler who wants very much to win, but who doesn't want to lose.

Those Catholics who decided for the laws of exception of 1893–1894 through the means of a majority are in no position to rebel when, by means of the same majority, the laws for the separation of church and state are decided.

Those socialists who want to pass the laws on workers' retirements by means of the majority are in no position to rebel against the same majority when it decides on some law that goes against their interests.

All parties that accept suffrage, however universal it might be, as the basis for their means of action cannot revolt as long as they are left the means of asserting themselves by the ballot.

Catholics, in general, are in this situation. The gentlemen in question in the late battles were "great electors," able to vote in senatorial elections; some were even parliamentarians. Not only had some voted and sought to be the majority in the chambers that prepare the laws, but the others had elaborated that law, had discussed its terms and articles.

Being parliamentarists, believers in the vote, the Catholics weren't logically consistent with themselves during their revolt.

The socialists are no more so. They speak constantly of social revolution, yet they spend all their time in puerile voting gestures in the perpetual search for a legal majority.

To accept the tutelage of the law yesterday, to reject it today, and to take it up again tomorrow, this is the way Catholics, socialists, and parliamentarists in general act. It is illogical.

None of their acts has a logical relation to that of the day before, no more than that of tomorrow will have one with that of today.

Either we accept the law of majorities or we don't accept it. Those who inscribe it in their program and seek to obtain the majority are illogical when they rebel against it.

This is how it is. But when Catholics or socialists revolt we don't seek the acts of yesterday; we don't worry about those that will be carried out tomorrow, we peacefully look on as the law is broken by its manufacturers.

It will be up to us to see to it that these days have no tomorrows.

So the anarchists alone are logical in revolt.

The anarchists don't vote. They don't want to be the majority that commands; they don't accept being the minority that obeys.

When they rebel they have no need to break any contract: they never accept binding their individuality to any government of any kind.

They alone, then, are rebels held back by no ties, and each of their violent gestures is related to their ideas, is logically consistent with their reasoning.

By demonstration, by observation, by experience or, lacking these, by force, by violence, these are the means by which the anarchists want to impose themselves. By majority, by the law, never!

[From *l'anarchie*, February 15, 1906.]

Fear

The bourgeois were frightened!!!

The bourgeois felt pass over them the wind of riot, the breath of revolt, and they feared the hurricane, the storm that would unleash those with unsatisfied appetites on their too-well-garnished tables.

The bourgeois were frightened!!!

The bourgeois, fat and tranquil, blissful and peaceful, heard the horrifying grumble of the painful and poor digestion of the thin, the rachitic, the unsatisfied. The bellies heard the rumblings of the arms, who refused to bring them their daily pittance.

The bourgeois were frightened!!!

The bourgeois gathered together their piles of money, their titles; they hid them in holes from the claws of the destroyers; the bourgeois stored their movable property, and they then looked around to see where to hide themselves. The big city wasn't very safe with all those threats in the air. And the countryside wasn't either. … When the evening came chateaus were being burned down there.

The bourgeois were frightened! A fear gripped their bellies, their stomachs, their throats, without any means of attenuating it presenting itself.

And so the bourgeois put up barricades of steel and blood in front of the workers, cemented with blood and flesh. They attempted to rejoice at seeing the little infantrymen and the heavy dragoons parade before their windows. They swooned before the handsome Republican Guards and the fine cavalrymen. And still, fear invaded their being. They were frightened.

That fear seemed to be mixed with remorse. One could believe that the bourgeois felt the logic of the acts that took in everyone and everything that they alone had possessed up till then.

The bourgeois were afraid that suddenly, in a great movement, the two sides of the scale that had always tilted in the direction of their desires would suddenly be leveled. They believed the moment for disgorgement had finally come. Since their lives were made of the deaths of other men, they believed that on this day the lives of others would be made of their deaths.

O anguished dream! The bourgeois were frightened, really frightened!!

But the hurricane passed over their heads and their bellies and didn't kill. The lightning rods of sabers and rifles sufficed for the few gusts that blew forgotten over society.

The worker again took up his labor. He again bent his back over the daily task. Today like yesterday, the slave prepares his master's swill.

The hurricane has passed … the bourgeois have slowly raised their heads. They looked upon their faces convulsed with fear … and they laughed. But their laugh was a snigger; their laugh was a bark.

Since he didn't know how to do his work himself, the hyenas and jackals were going to fall on the lion, caught in the trap of his ignorance and confidence.

The women who, in 1871, poked out the eyes of Communards with their parasols have had children. These children are now in the magistracy, in the administration, in the army. The wear the kepi or the robe; they kill with the Code, regulations, or the sword; but they kill without pity.

The bourgeois were frightened.

They are taking revenge for having been frightened!!! Like a club, the jackhammer of justice is descending on the vanquished. The Magnauds and the Bulots, the Séré de Rivières and the Bridoisons, all of them are in agreement in harshly striking the troublemakers.[2]

Never have those who do not labor felt such respect for those who labor. Hindering the freedom to work means months and months of prison. Men have been sentenced until the healing of their wounds, children to reform schools, and adolescents to the penal brigades. Those who reason must be put down.

The bourgeois were frightened!!!

---

2   Judges and officers, including the fictitious Bridoison, from Beaumarchais's *Marriage of Figaro*. —ed.

But those who must be struck the hardest are the enemies of all the bourgeois, both the reactionary and the socialist bourgeois: the anarchists.

Other men are defeated by the weight of their own ignorance; it will still be quite a while before they free themselves from their foolishness. But the anarchists are defeated by the ignorance and passivity of others, so they work every day to educate them, to make rebels of them. It is thus they who are the danger; it is they who must be struck.

The bourgeois want to avenge themselves, but they are cowards, and so it is the bystanders they strike. They fear the might of anarchist logic, and they know that the sophistry of their reasoning will burst like soap bubbles in the sun. They can crush us with the dead weight of the brutal force of numbers, but they know that we will always defeat them in reason's combat.

"That man had an anarchist paper in his pocket!—That one had pamphlets on sociology.—That one had needles on him." And they strike even harder whoever dares read anything but *La Croix*, *La Petite République*, or *Le Petit Journal*.

Why don't you strike the authors, the publishers of these publications? Are they untouchable, above all laws, or are you afraid of finding yourselves confronting the truth, viscous Berengers of politics?[3]

Bourgeois, you were frightened!!!

And it was nothing but a shadow that passed across the heaven of your beatitude. But be on your guard: it's only when it's about to erupt that you will see the storm that will swallow you up. It won't be announced by tiny lightning bolts. It will surge around you and you will be no more.

Bourgeois, you experience the frisson of fear, and you are savoring the joy of revenge. … But don't be in such a hurry to celebrate. Don't exaggerate too greatly the reprisals of your victory, for the upcoming revolt could very well not leave you the time to be frightened. …

---

3   Name of the leader of a medieval band of brigands. —ed.

The bourgeois were frightened!!!

[From *l'anarchie*, May 17, 1906.]

Spineless Meat

We in Paris, almost without our knowledge, were threatened with a great revolution.

We were threatened with great perturbations in the slaughterhouses of La Villette.

A few snatches of the reasons for this were allowed to reach indiscreet ears. Hoof and mouth were spoken of. But what is this alongside other reasons, ones we must know nothing of.

Only dead meat should leave the slaughterhouses of the city, and only living meat should enter.

But go see. Beasts enter, pulled on, pushed against. They must enter alive, with a breath, only a breath, hardly anything.

And the contaminated carrion is sold, served to the faubourgs of Paris from Ménilmontant to Montrouge, from Belleville to La Chapelle.

Go, workers of the slaughterhouses, defend your "rights." Go, butcher boys, defend "your own." You must go on slaughtering, go on serving poisoned meat.

Go cattle-drivers, turn and re-turn your fever-bearing meats from the Beauce to Paris, from Paris to all the workers from the north, the west, and the east. Go ahead, come to Paris, contaminate your animals or bring here the poison contracted elsewhere.

What do evil gestures, useless gestures, poisonous gestures matter? One must live. And to work is to poison, to pillage, to steal, to lie to other men. Work means adulterating drinks, manufacturing cannons, slaughtering and serving slices of poisoned meat.

That's what work means for the spineless meat that surrounds us, the meat that should be slaughtered and pushed into the sewers.

[From *l'anarchie*, August 2, 1906.]

ÉMILE ARMAND

Émile Armand followed a strange path to the world of anarchist individualism, but once he arrived there, he was a dominant figure for decades. Born in 1872, he never attended school, obtaining an education in his father's library, later boasting that when he was thirteen, he was capable of learning a language in its entirety in three months.

As a late teen, he read the New Testament from beginning to end, which so moved him that he became an officer in the Salvation Army, where he remained for a few years until, after reading his first anarchist texts in Jean Grave's newspaper, Les Temps Nouveaux, *he developed his own ideas on a Tolstoyan Christian anarchism, which he propagated in his newspaper,* L'Ère Nouvelle. *The Christian part of his doctrine was soon jettisoned, and in 1902 he helped Libertad found the Causeries Populaires. He had moved so far from his Salvation Army past that in short order he was arrested for two common individualist crimes: counterfeiting and complicity in desertion. He published a steady flow of newspapers, all with titles that defined their contents:* Hors du Troupeau *(Outside the Herd),* Les Refractaires *(The Insubordinate),* Pendant la Mêlée *(During the Fray), and* Par delà la Mêlée *(Above the Fray), the latter two published during World War I.*

He was sentenced to five years imprisonment in 1918 for abetting desertion and upon his release in 1922 started yet another newspaper, L'Endehors *(The Outsider), whose title he borrowed from the newspaper of the eccentric anarchist, Zo d'Axa.*

Armand, more than almost any other leading figure of individualism, focused attention on the sex question; he believed in absolutely no inhibitions on sex impulses, advocating any combination consenting individuals desire. He also developed the concept of "amorous comradeship," in which political comradeship, in order to be complete, required consummation.

Never wavering an inch from his focus on the individual, he said at the Amsterdam anarchist conference of 1907 that "to demand that all anarchists have a similar vision of anarchism is demanding the impossible. ... Anarchism is not strictly a philosophical doctrine, it's a life." And believing in the full liberty of the individual, even in the face of his own propaganda work, he was quoted by his anarchist individualist friend Mauricius in a memorial article as saying, "I don't remember who first said, 'I expose, I propose, I don't impose.' This is a lovely formula and Armand made it his own and repeated it often."

His long anarchist life ended in 1962.

Is the Anarchist Ideal Realizable?

Is the anarchist ideal realizable?

I am embarrassed as to how to properly respond to the investigation of *La Revue Anarchiste*. Is there an anarchist ideal? Is anarchism an ideal? If there is an anarchist ideal, what is it, since there are several tendencies and currents within anarchism?

It is true that the follow-up to the question posed by *La Revue Anarchiste* seems to delimit or define the anarchist ideal: "without authority," "suppression of all constraints."

We should doubtless read "of all political authority," of "all constraints of a statist or governmental order or anything having to do with them," for we know that biologically speaking, man isn't free: he is subject to the directives of his determinism.

Being an anarchist means denying, rejecting the *arche:* political and legal domination, the apparatus of power. But it's even more: it means denying, rejecting the utility of the state in ordering relations between men. Better, it means doing without the intervention and the protection of *archist* institutions in reaching agreement with others.

How can I know if in the future "man" will be able to do without political authority, of any imposed authority? How can I know if the "suppression of all constraints" will ever be anything but the prerogative of tiny minorities? Judging by appearances, I see no man who does without authority; I see no minority escaping from "all" constraints.

In fact, I don't really care.

I feel that I am an anarchist, and that's enough. I feel myself to be hindered, blocked, tied down, limited, restrained by the multiple bonds forged by state institutions. I rebel against these constraints; I escape from them as soon as I find the occasion to do so. When I have to deal with an ordinary human being I almost always find him to be imbued with conventional ideas, prejudices, beliefs, commitments, points of view inculcated in him by the agents of *archism*. I attempt to liberate those I encounter from these foreign suggestions.

Alas, I don't live "without authority." At every corner, at every crossroad I must suffer from its visible representation. And if only this was all there was. Even so, in my daily relations with antistatists like myself I do my best to get along with others by ignoring the game of governmental institutions. I more or less succeed in doing this, but I persevere. And I pay little attention to whether or not the relations I maintain with "my people" square with education, economic or sexual morality, or the teachings of the state or church (the stand-in for the state).

And now let us come to individualist anarchism.

Anarchist individualism is not an ideal, but an activity. A state of open or hidden—but continuous—struggle against any theory of life that subordinates the individual to governmental authority, that considers him in function of the state, that judges him by social constraints and legal sanctions whose legitimacy in relation to his personal development he never could and cannot weigh.

I don't know if those who constitute it form an "elite," but I maintain that throughout the world there exists an individualist anarchist milieu, a milieu of "comrades" that, by all the means in its power, works at ignoring the social, moral, intellectual conditions upon which *archist* society rest, using ruse if open escape isn't possible.

We don't live on hypotheses or conjectures. If there is an anarchist ideal, I propose to realize all of it that I can immediately, without waiting, without asking if I am a member or not of an elite, doing so by associating myself with atheist, materialist, pleasure-seeking comrades, in a hurry to go full steam ahead, just as I am. Everything else is a distraction or metaphysics.

We thank *La Revue Anarchiste* for having given us the occasion to enjoy ourselves among comrades.

[From *La Revue Anarchiste*, 1930.]

Principal Tendencies and Theses of the "Unique" Center

Individual Culture and Education

Life as will and responsibility

Violence (the ideology of domination, imposition, exploitation, etc.) as the origin of wars

Reciprocity as the ethic of sociability

While waiting for a world where suffering will have been reduced to a tiny minimum, its elimination from relations conditioned by friendship and camaraderie

Fidelity to the word given and to the clauses of pacts freely consented to, and this in all domains

Voluntary and contractual associationism, cooperatism, and mutualism in all branches of human activity

Liberation from prejudices concerning race, external appearance, inequality of sexes and social conditions, et cetera.

Personal life as a work of art

The noninterference in the sphere of activity of others determining the limits to the expansion of the personality

Reasoned Eugenics and Thought-Out Naturism

Combat against prostitution in all its forms and against the idea of the woman considered solely as a "physiological necessity"

Sensitivity, the spirit of understanding and reconciliation, the fight against the attitude of "too-bad-for-you" as facts of internal vitality

Practice of "first clean up in front of your door" before getting involved in the affairs of others

Interest in free circles, libertarian colonies, innovative schools

Pluralism in friendship, exclusive of preferences and privileges

In case of special attention in one particular direction, this latter will always be in favor of he who has suffered most because of the spreading or realization of one, another, or several of the above theses.

[From an undated flyer from the Amis de E. Armand, c. 1944.]

On Sexual Freedom

When the individualists call for sexual freedom, what do they mean? Do they demand the freedom to rape or of debauchery? Do they aspire to the obliteration of sentiment in love life, to the disappearance of attachment, tenderness, or affection? Do they glorify unthinking promiscuity or bestial sexual satisfaction, both in time and outside of time? Not in the least. In demanding sexual freedom they simply want the possibility for every individual to dispose of his sexual life as he wishes and in whatever circumstances, in keeping with the qualities of temperament, sentiment, and reason that are particular to him. Note that I say "his" sex life, which doesn't imply that of others. Nor do they demand a freedom in sexual life that will not have been preceded by sex education. On the contrary, they believe that gradually, in the period preceding puberty, human beings must be left in ignorance about nothing concerning sexual life—in other words the ineluctable attraction of the sexes—viewed from either the sentimental, the emotional, or the physiological point of view.

And so, freedom of sexual life is not synonymous with debauch, in other words, "loss of sexual sensitivity." Sexual freedom is exclusively of an individual order. It presupposes an education of the will allowing every individual to determine *for himself* the point where he ceases to be the master of his passions or penchants, an education that is perhaps more instinctive than it at first might appear. Like all freedoms, that of the sexual life involves an effort, not of abstinence—abstention is a mark of moral insufficiency, just as debauchery is a sign of moral weakness—but of judgment, of discernment, of classification. In other words, it's not a question of the quantity or the number of experiences, but of the quality of the person who experiences. In conclusion, the freedom of sexual life remains united, in the individualist meaning, to preparatory sexual education and the power of individual determination.

Aspects of Sexual Life

The individualist is able to differentiate between sexual freedom and sexual disorder. "Sexual freedom" and "free love" rest on a conscious, reasoned choice, though they exclude neither sentimental impulsiveness nor emotional investigation. In the domain of the sensual, unreasoned sexual promiscuity betrays a lesser effort, a loss of the power of individual determination. Of course, reasoned promiscuity can be appropriate to certain temperaments, to certain characters, but it is irrational to extend it to all. The companion who believes she has to surrender to no matter which "comrade" from individualist or anarchist duty would in no way be an individualist or an anarchist because she would believe herself to be in the grip of an obligation.

Free love includes, and sexual freedom implies, a number of varieties adapted to the various amorous or affective temperaments, constant, flighty, tender, passionate, voluptuous, etc., and assumes a variety of forms, varying from simple monogamy to simultaneous plurality; temporary or stable couples, ménages of several individuals, polygenic or polyandrous; single or plural unions ignorant of cohabitation; central affections based on affinities of an order more sentimental or intellectual around which gravitate friendships; and relations of a character more sensual, more voluptuous, more capricious. They don't pay attention to degrees of family relations and are perfectly willing to accept that a sexual tie could unite even very close relatives. Only one thing matters, that everyone should find satisfaction, and since sensual pleasure and tenderness are aspects of the joy of life, all should live their sensual or sentimental life to the full, making those around them happy. The individualist wants nothing else.

There are people who don't understand that a mature man could be in love with a young woman. Or reciprocally, that a young woman could be in love with a man who has reached the autumn of his life. This is a prejudice. There are years when the fall is so beautiful that the trees flower anew. There are even certain human beings who still have an amorous temperament until the next-to-last dawn of their existence, which is every bit as fresh and spontaneous as the first one in their youth. A being who has arrived at his autumn can possess natural gifts that engender seduction, for example, he can be made attractive by a past that is adventurous and out of the ordinary.

Those who have experienced and felt much in the realm of sexual sensuality are perhaps more qualified to initiate young people, for they usually proceed with a delicacy and gentleness unknown to the ardor of adolescence.

What is more, sexual needs are more pressing in certain periods of individual life than at others. There are phases of personal existence where tenderness and attachment have a higher price than pure sensual satisfaction. It is the observation of all these nuances that constitutes applied free love, the practice of sexual freedom. Like all stages of individualist life, free love and sexual freedom are an experience from which each can draw the conclusions most appropriate to his own emancipation.

[From Émile Armand, *Initiation individualiste
anarchiste*, 1923.]

What Is an Anarchist?

A chaos of beings, of acts and ideas; a disordered, bitter, merciless struggle; a perpetual lie, a blindly spinning wheel, one day placing someone at the pinnacle, and the next day crushing him: these are just a few of the images that describe current society, if it were possible for it to be depicted. The brush of the greatest of painters and the pen of the greatest of writers would splinter like glass if we were to employ them to express even a distant echo of the tumult and melee that is depicted by the clash of appetites, aspirations, hatreds, and devotions that collide and mix together the different categories among which men are parceled out.

Who will ever precisely express the unfinished battle between private interests and collective needs? The sentiments of individuals and the logic of generalities? All of this makes up current society, and none of this suffices to describe it. A minority that possesses the faculty to produce and consume and the possibility to parasitically exist in a thousand different forms: fixed and movable property, capital as tools or as funds, capital as teaching and capital as education.

Facing it is an immense majority, which possesses nothing but its arms or brains or other productive organs that it is forced to rent, lease, or prostitute, not only in order to procure what it needs in order not to die of hunger, but also to permit the small number of holders of power or property or exchange values to live more or less in luxury at its expense. A mass rich and poor, slaves of immemorial, hereditary prejudices, some because this is in their interest, others because they are sunk in ignorance or don't want to escape it. A multitude whose cult is that of money and the prototype of the rich man, the rule of the mediocre incapable of both great vices and great virtues. And the mass of degenerates on high and down low, without profound aspirations, without any other goal than that of arriving at a position of pleasure and ease, even if it means crushing, if necessary, the friends of yesterday, [who have] become the downtrodden of today.

A provisional state that ceaselessly threatens to transform itself into a definitive one, and a definitive state that threatens to never be anything but provisional. Lives that give the lie to espoused convictions, and convictions that serve as a springboard for crooked ambitions. Free thinkers who show themselves to be more clericalist than the clerical, and believers who show themselves to be coarse materialists. The superficial individual who wants to pass for profound, and the profound individual who doesn't succeed in being taken seriously. No one would deny that this is a portrait of society, and no thinking person could fail to see that this painting does not even begin to depict reality. Why? Because there is a mask placed before every face; because no one cares to *be*, because all aspire only to seem. To seem: this is the supreme ideal, and if we so avidly desire ease and wealth, it is in order to seem, since only money now allows us to make an impression.

This mania, this passion, this race for appearances, for what it can procure them, devours both the rich man and the vagabond, the most erudite and the illiterate. The worker who curses his foreman wishes to become one in turn; the merchant who judges his commercial honor to be of an unequalled price doesn't hesitate to carry out dishonorable deals; the small shop owner, member of patriotic and nationalist electoral committees, hastens to transmit his orders to foreign manufacturers as soon as he finds this profitable. The socialist lawyer, advocate of the poverty-stricken proletariat herded into the malodorous parts of the city, passes his vacations in a chateau or resides in the wealthy neighborhoods of the city, where fresh air is abundant. The free thinker still willingly marries in church, and often has his children baptized there. The religious man doesn't dare express his ideas, since ridiculing religion is the done thing. Where is sincerity to be found? The gangrene has spread everywhere. We find it in the family, where father, mother, and children often hate and deceive each other while saying that they love each other, while leading each other to believe that they feel affection for each other. We see it at work in the couple, where the husband and wife not meant for each other betray each other, not daring to break the ties that bind them. It is there for all to see in groups, where each seeks to supplant his neighbor in the esteem of the president, the secretary, or the treasurer, while waiting to assume their place when they no longer need them. It abounds in the acts of devotion, in public doings, in private conversations, in official harangues. To seem! To seem! To seem pure, disinterested, and generous, while at the same time we consider purity, disinterest, and generosity to be vain foolishness; to seem moral, honest, and virtuous when probity, virtue, and morality are the least concerns of those who profess them.

Where can one find a person who escapes corruption, who consents not to seem?

We don't claim to have ever met such a person. We note that sincere, eminently sincere individuals are rare. We affirm that the number of human beings who work disinterestedly is quite limited. Right or wrong, I have more respect for the individual who cynically admits to wanting to enjoy life by profiting from others than for the liberal and philanthropic bourgeois whose lips resound with grandiose words, but whose fortune is built on the concealed exploitation of the unfortunate.

It will be objected that we are allowing ourselves to be led by our indignation. That, in the first place, nothing proves that our anger and invective are not also a way of seeming. Be on your guard: what you will find here are observations, opinions, theses; it will be left to the reader to determine what they are worth. The pages that follow are not marked with the seal of infallibility. We don't seek to convert anyone to our point of view. Our goal is to make those who browse these pages reflect, with the right to accept or reject that which is not in accord with their own convictions.

It will be objected that this is dealing with the question at too high a level, or from a metaphysical point of view; that we must descend to the level of concrete reality. The reality is this: that current society is the result of a long historical process, perhaps still just beginning; that humanity—or the different humanities—are simply at the point of seeking or preparing their way, that they are groping and stumbling; that they lose their way, find it again, advance, retreat, lose their way; that they are at times shaken to their foundation by certain crises, dragged along, cast on destiny's road and then slow down or march in place; that by scratching the polish, the varnish, the surface of contemporary civilizations we would lay bare the stammering, the childishness, and the superstitions of the prehistoric. Who denies this? We accept that all these things render the "human problem" singularly complex.

Finally, it will be objected that it is folly to seek to discover, to establish the responsibility of the individual; that he is submerged, absorbed in his environment; that his ideas reflect the ideas and his acts the acts of those around him; that it can't be otherwise, and if from the top to the bottom of the social ladder it is "seeming" and not "being" that is the aspiration, the fault is that of the current stage of general evolution and not that of the individual, the member of society, a minuscule atom lost in a formidable aggregate.

We answer honestly that we don't intend to write for all the beings who make up society. Let us be understood: we address ourselves to those who think or are in the process of thinking, to those who have grown impatient with waiting for the mass, which can't or won't think; to those who can't adapt to appearances and to those whom the current stage of society doesn't satisfy.

We write for the curious, for thinkers, for the critical—for those who aren't content with formulas or empty solutions.

It's either the one or the other: either there's nothing else to be done than to allow the inevitable evolution to run its course, to bow in a cowardly fashion before circumstances, to passively witness the parade of events and admit that while waiting for something better all is for the best in the best of societies. Our theses and opinions will not interest those who share this way of seeing things. Alternatively, without arming yourself with an exaggerated optimism, you can step off the main roads, withdraw to a great height, question yourself, and look into yourself for the roots of our own malaise. We address ourselves to those not satisfied with the current society, to those who are thirsty for real life, for real activity and find around themselves only the artificial and the unreal. There are those who are thirsty for harmony and ask themselves why disorder and fratricidal struggles abound around them. ...

Let us conclude: the spirit that reflects and attentively considers men and things encounters in the complex of things we call society a nearly insurmountable barrier to truly free, independent, individual life. This is enough for him to qualify it as evil, and for him to wish for its disappearance.

[From *Brochure Mensuelle*, no. 26,
February 1925.]

Is the Illegalist Anarchist Our Comrade?

And when we regard the thief in himself, we cannot say that we find him less human than other classes of society. The sentiment of large bodies of thieves is highly communistic among themselves; and if they thus represent a survival from an earlier age, they might also be looked upon as the precursors of a better age in the future. They have their pals in every town, with runs and refuges always open,

and are lavish and generous to a degree to their
own kind. And if they look upon the rich as their
natural enemies and fair prey, a view which it might
be difficult to gainsay, many of them at any rate are
animated by a good deal of the Robin Hood spirit,
and are really helpful to the poor.

  (Edward Carpenter: *Civilization, Its
  Cause and Cure*)

I am not a supporter of illegalism. I am an *alegal*. Illegalism is a
dangerous last resort for he who engages in it, even temporarily,
a last resort that should neither be preached nor advocated. But
the question I propose to study is not that of asking whether or
not an illegal trade is perilous or not, but rather if the anarchist
who earns his daily bread by resorting to trades condemned by
the police and tribunals is right or wrong to expect that an anarchist who accepts working for a boss will treat him as a comrade,
a comrade whose point of view we defend in broad daylight and
who we don't deny when he falls into the grips of the police or
the decisions of judges. (Unless he asks us to remain silent about
his case.)

  The illegalist anarchist in fact doesn't want us to treat him like
a "poor relation" who we don't dare publicly admit to because this
would do harm to the anarchist cause, or because not separating
ourselves from him when the representatives of capitalist vengeance come crushing down on him would risk losing the sympathy of syndicalists and the clientele of petit-bourgeois anarchist
sympathizers for the anarchist movement.

  The illegalist anarchist expressly addresses his comrade who is
exploited by a boss, that is, *who feels himself* to be exploited. He
hardly expects to be understood by those who work at a job that
is to their taste. He places among the latter the anarchist doctri-
naires and propagandists who spread, defend, and expose ideas in
accordance their opinions—this is what we hope, at least. Even if
they only receive a pitiful, a very pitiful salary for their labor, their
moral situation isn't comparable to the position of an anarchist
working under the surveillance of a foreman and obliged to suffer

all day the promiscuity of people whose company is antagonistic to him. This is why the illegalist anarchist denies to those who have jobs that please them the right to cast judgment on his profession on the margins of the law.

All those who do written or spoken propaganda work that is to their taste, all those who work at a profession they like too often forget that they are privileged in comparison with the mass of humanity, their comrades, those who are forced to put on their harness every morning, from January first to the next New Year's Eve, and work at tasks for which they have no liking.[1]

The illegalist anarchist claims he is every bit as much a comrade as the merchant, the secretary at town hall, or the dancing master, none of whom in any way modify—and certainly to no greater degree than he—the economic conditions of current society. A lawyer, a doctor, a teacher can send articles to an anarchist newspaper and give talks at tiny libertarian circles all they want; they nevertheless remain both the supporters and the supported of the *archist* system, which gave them the monopoly that permits them to exercise their profession and the regulations to which they are obliged to submit if they want to continue working at their trades.

It is not an exaggeration to say that any anarchist who accepts being exploited for the profit of a private boss or the state boss is committing an act of treason against anarchist ideas. He is, in effect, reinforcing domination and exploitation, is contributing to maintaining the existence of *archism*. It is doubtless true that becoming aware of his inconsistency he strives to redeem or repair his conduct by making propaganda. But whatever the propaganda done by the exploited, he still remains an accomplice of the exploiters, a cooperator in the system of exploitation that rules the conditions under which production takes place.

---

1   One day in Brussels, I discussed the question with Élisée Reclus. He said, in conclusion: "I work at something that pleases me; I don't see where I have the right to judge those who don't want to work at something that doesn't please them." [Note in the original. —ed.]

This is why it is not accurate to say that the anarchist "who works," who submits to the system of domination and exploitation in place, is a victim. He is an accomplice as much as he is a victim. All of the exploited, legal or illegal, cooperate in the state of domination. There is no difference between the anarchist worker who earned 175,000 or 200,000 francs in thirty years of labor and who has purchased a hut in the country with his savings and the illegalist anarchist who grabs a safe containing 200,000 francs and with this sum acquires a house by the seaside. Both are anarchists in word only, it is true, but the difference between them is that the anarchist worker submits to the terms of the economic contract that the leaders of the social milieu impose on him, while the anarchist thief *does not submit to them.*

The law protects the exploited as much as the exploiter, the dominated as much as the dominator in their mutual social relations, and as long as he submits the anarchist is as well protected in his property and his person as the *archist.* The law makes no distinction between the *archist* and the anarchist as long as both accept the injunctions of the social contract. Whether they will or not, the anarchists who submit, the bosses, workers, employees, and functionaries, have the public forces, tribunals, social conventions, and official educators on their side. This is the reward for their submission: when they constrain—by moral persuasion or the force of the law—the *archist* employer to pay his anarchist employee, the forces of social preservation could care less that deep down, or even on the outside, the wage earner is hostile to the wage system.

On the contrary, the opponent of, the rebel against the social contract, the illegalist anarchist has against him *the entire social organization* when in order to "live his life" he leaps over all intermediary stages in order to immediately reach the goal that the submissive anarchist will reach only later, if ever. He runs an enormous risk, and it is only fair that this risk be compensated for by immediate results, if there are results at all.

Resorting to ruse, which the illegalist anarchist constantly practices, is a procedure employed by all revolutionaries. Secret societies are an aspect of this. In order to put up subversive posters we wait for policemen to walk in another sector. An anarchist who leaves for America conceals his moral, political, and philosophical point of view. Whatever he might be, apparently submissive or openly rebellious, the anarchist is always an illegal as regards the law. When he propagates his anarchist ideas he contravenes the special laws that repress anarchist propaganda; even more, by his anarchist mentality he opposes himself to the written law itself in its essence, for the law is the concretion of *archism*.[2]

The rebellious anarchist cannot fail to be found sympathetic by the submissive anarchist who feels himself to be submissive. In his illegal attitude the anarchist who either couldn't or wouldn't break with legality recognizes himself, realized logically. The temperament, the reflections of the submissive anarchist can lead him to disapprove certain acts of the rebellious anarchist, but can never render him personally antipathetic.[3]

The illegalist answers the revolutionary anarchist who reproaches him with immediately seeking his financial well-being by saying that he, the revolutionary, does nothing different. The

---

2   Though I don't have the statistics required, a reading of anarchist newspapers indicates that the number of those justly or unjustly condemned—imprisoned, sent to penal colonies, or gunned down—for revolutionary anarchist agitation (including "propaganda by the deed") is far greater than those justly or unjustly condemned, or gunned down, for illegalism. The theoreticians of revolutionary anarchism bear a large part of the responsibility for these condemnations, for they have never couched the propaganda in support of revolutionary acts with the same reservations that the serious "explainers" of the illegalist act provide for the practice of illegalism. [Note in the original. —ed.]

3   The anarchist whose illegalism attacks the state or known exploiters has never indisposed "the worker" concerning anarchism. I was in Amiens during the trial of Jacob, who often attacked colonial officers. Thanks to the explanations in "Germinal" the workers of Amiens were quite sympathetic to Jacob and the ideas of individual expropriation. Even the nonanarchist, the illegal who attacks a banker, a factory owner, a manufacturer, a treasurer, a postal wagon, and so forth, is found sympathetic by the exploited, who consider as valets or squealers those wage earners who defend the coin or the cash of their boss, private or state. I have noted this hundreds of times. [Note in the original. —ed.]

economic revolutionary expects from the revolution an improvement in his personal economic situation: if not, he wouldn't be a revolutionary. The revolution will give him what he hoped for or it won't, just as an illegal operation furnishes or doesn't furnish what was counted on to the person who executes it. It's simply a question of dates. Even when the economic question is not a factor, one only makes a revolution if one expects a personal benefit, a religious, political, intellectual, or perhaps ethical benefit. Every revolutionary is an egoist.

* * *

Does the explanation of acts of "expropriation" committed by illegalists have an unfavorable influence, in general and in particular, on anarchist propaganda?

In order to answer this question, which is the most important of all questions, one must not lose sight for a single second of the fact that in coming into the world, or in entering any country, the human unit finds economic conditions that are imposed on it. Whatever one's opinions, one must, in order to live (or die) in peace, submit to constraint. Where there is constraint the contract is no longer valid, since it is unilateral, and bourgeois codes themselves admit that a commitment made when the signatory is threatened is of no legal value. The anarchist thus finds himself in a state of legitimate defense against the executors and the partisans of the imposed economic contract. For example, we have never heard an anarchist, exercising an illegal trade, call for a society based on universal banditry. His situation, his acts, are solely in relation to the economic contract that the capitalists or the unilaterals impose even on those revolted by its clauses. The illegalism of anarchists is only transitory: a last resort.

If the social milieu granted anarchists the inalienable possession of their personal means of production; if they could freely, and without any fiscal restriction (taxes, customs duties), dispose of their products; if they allowed an exchange value to be employed among them that would be struck with no tax, all of this at their own risk, illegalism, in my sense of the word (that is, economic illegalism), would no longer be understood. Economic illegalism is thus purely accidental.[4]

In any event, economic or otherwise, illegalism is a function of legalism. The day authority disappears—political, intellectual, and economic authority—the illegalists will also disappear.

It is on this path that we must orient ourselves in order for illegalist acts to benefit anarchist propaganda.

Every anarchist, submissive or not, considers all those among his like who refuse to accept military servitude to be comrades. It is inexplicable, then, why his attitude would change when it's a matter of refusing to serve economically.

We can easily understand that anarchists don't want to contribute to the economic life of a country that doesn't accord them the possibility of explaining themselves by the pen or the spoken word and that limits their faculties and their possibilities of realization and association, in whatever realm. At the same time they, for their part, would allow nonanarchists to conduct themselves however they wish. Those anarchists who agree to participate in the economic functioning of societies where they cannot live according to their desires are inconsistent. We can't understand why they object to those who rebel against this state of things.

The rebel against economic servitude finds himself forced, *from the instinct for preservation*, by the need and the will to life, to appropriate the production of others. This instinct is not only primordial, it is legitimate, the illegalists affirm, compared to capitalist accumulation, accumulation that the capitalist, taken personally, does not require in order to exist, accumulation that is a superfluity. Now, who are these "others" whom the reasoning illegalist attacks, the anarchist who exercises an illegal profession. The "others" are those who want majorities to dominate or oppress minorities; they are the partisans of the domination or the dictatorship of one class or caste over others; they are the voters, the supporters of the state, of the monopolies and privileges it

---

4   Socially speaking, on the day when the costs of keeping a property will be superior to what it brings in, property, daughter of exploitation, will disappear. [Note in the original. —ed.]

implies. In reality, for the anarchist these "others" are enemies, irreconcilable adversaries. The moment he economically lays into him, the illegalist anarchist no longer sees in him, cannot see in him, anything but an instrument of the *archist* system.

These explanations provided, we can't say that the illegalist anarchist is wrong who considers himself betrayed when those anarchists who preferred following less perilous roads than his abandon or don't care to explain their attitudes.

* * *

I repeat what I said when I began these lines: since there is a last resort, that offered by illegalism is the most dangerous of all, and it must be demonstrated that it brings in more than it costs, which is something quite exceptional. The illegalist anarchist who is thrown in prison has no favors to hope for as far as probation or reduction of his sentence. As the saying goes, his dossier is marked in red. But with this caveat, it must still be pointed out that in order to be seriously practiced, illegalism demands a steely temperament, a sureness of oneself that doesn't belong to everyone. It is to be feared that the practices of illegalist anarchism, as with all experiences in anarchist life that don't march in step with the routines of daily existence, take control of the will and thought of the illegalist to such an extent that they render him incapable of any other activity, any other attitude. The same also goes for certain legal trades that spare those who practice them the need to be at a factory or an office.

Conclusions

Economic anarchists and economic leaders and rulers *impose* working conditions on workers that are incompatible with the anarchist notion of life—that is, with the absence of exploitation of man by man. In principle an anarchist refuses to allow working conditions to be imposed on him or to allow himself to be exploited. It is only by abdicating responsibility or surrendering that he accepts them.

And there is no difference between submitting to the payment of taxes, submitting to exploitation, and submitting to military service.

It is understood that the majority of anarchists submit. "We obtain more from legality by getting around it, by fooling it, than by confronting it face-to-face." This is true. But the anarchist who ruses with the law has no reason to brag about it. In doing this he escapes the dangerous consequences of draft-dodging, the penal colony, that "most abject of slaveries." But if he doesn't have to suffer all this, the submissive anarchist has to deal with "professional deformation": by externally conforming to the law, a number of anarchists finish by no longer reacting at all and pass to the other side of the barricades. An exceptional temperament is necessary in order to ruse with the law without allowing oneself to be caught up in the net of legality.

As for the anarchist-producer in the current economic milieu: this is a myth. Where are the anarchists who produce antiauthoritarian values? By their productivity almost all anarchists collaborate in maintaining the current economic state of affairs. You'll never make me believe that the anarchist who builds prisons, barracks, and churches; who manufactures arms, munitions, and uniforms; who prints codes, political journals, and religious books; and who stocks them, transports them, and sells them is participating in antiauthoritarian production. Even the anarchist who produces necessary items for the use of voters and the elected is false to his convictions.

It is not up to either verbal propagandists or men of the pen to accuse obscure individualists of materially benefiting from their ideas. Do they count as nothing the "moral" and sometimes pecuniary benefit their efforts procure for them? Renown spreads their names "from one end of the earth to the other"; they have disciples, translators, slanderers, persecutors. For what do they count all this?

I find it only fair that every form of labor receives a salary in all domains. It is fair that if you suffer for your opinions you should also profit from them. What matters is that this profit not be realized by violence, trickery, ruse, theft, fraud, or imposition of any kind to the detriment or harm or wrong of one's comrades, of those from "our world."

In the current social milieu anarchism extends from Tolstoy to Bonnot. Warren, Proudhon, Kropotkin, Ravachol, Caserio, Louise Michel, Libertad, Pierre Chardon, Tchorny, the tendencies they represent or that are represented by certain living animators or inspirations whose names are of little importance are like the nuances of a rainbow where each individual chooses the tint that most pleases his vision.

In assuming the strictly individualist anarchist point of view—and it is with this that I will conclude—the criterion for camaraderie doesn't reside in the fact that one is an office worker, factory worker, functionary, newspaper seller, smuggler, or thief, it resides in this, that legal or illegal, *my* comrade will in the first place seek to sculpt his own individuality, to spread antiauthoritarian ideas wherever he can, and finally, by rendering life among those who share his ideas as agreeable as possible, will reduce useless and avoidable suffering to as negligible a quantity as possible.

[From *L'Illégaliste anarchiste, est-il notre camarade?*
Paris and Orleans: Editions de l'en-dehors, 1911.]

MARIUS JACOB

Marius Jacob was only twelve years old when he left home as a cabin boy in 1891 on a long-distance voyage. Just four years later, barely sixteen years old, he was already a typesetter and an anarchist militant. In those years just after the wave of terrorist bombings from 1892 to 1894, Jacob remained attracted to the tactic and fell into a trap set by an agent provocateur who offered to buy him materials to fabricate an explosive device. Unable to find work upon his release from prison because the police had informed prospective employers of his past and beliefs, he embarked on a life of illegalism.

Arrested after robbing the municipal pawn shop of Marseilles, he escaped from prison in 1899 and returned to his life of crime, but crime with a distinct difference. He formed an organized band of anarchist criminals, the Night Workers, whose acts of individual reappropriation were only carried out "at the homes of social parasites: priests, officers, judges, etc." He refused to harm those he considered useful: "doctors, architects, litterateurs, etc." Unlike some later illegalists, in particular the killers of the Bonnot Gang, he forbade killing except as a last resort in self-defense, as occurred at his final crime in Amiens on April 21, 1903. In addition, the profits of all thefts were tithed, with 10 percent of all takings going to the cause.

When finally captured, he admitted to having his hand in 106 crimes across France, Belgium, and Italy. At his trial in 1905 he remained a defiant anarchist. When the president of the tribunal told him to stand up, he answered, "No, sir." When told to take off his hat, he told the judge, "You have yours on."

Sentenced to life imprisonment on the penal colony of Cayenne, he remained an anarchist like no other, maintaining a voluminous and touching correspondence with his mother. In 1925, thanks to a massive campaign in his favor, he was released from penal servitude and returned to France, where he worked as a traveling hat-and-clothing salesman and continued his anarchist activities.

In 1954 he committed suicide, taking with him his beloved dog. He wrote in his suicide note, "I leave you without despair, a smile on my lips, peace in my heart. ... I lived, I can die." The revolutionary syndicalist newspaper Révolution Prolétarienne *declared in the headline for its article on his death, "The Last French Anarchist Is Dead."*

Why I Stole

Messieurs:

You now know who I am: a rebel living off the products of his burglaries. In addition, I burned down several hotels and defended my freedom against the aggressions of the agents of power.

I laid bare to you my entire existence as a combatant: I submit it as a problem for your intelligence.

Not recognizing anyone's right to judge me, I ask for neither pardon nor indulgence. I don't go begging to those I hate and scorn. You are the stronger. Dispose of me as you wish; send me to a penal colony or the gallows. I don't care! But before going our separate ways let me tell you one last thing.

Since you mainly condemn me for being a thief, it's useful to define what theft is.

In my opinion theft is a need to take that is felt by all men in order to satisfy their appetites. This need manifests itself in everything: from the stars that are born and die like living beings, to the insect in space, so small, so minuscule that our eyes can barely distinguish it. Life is nothing but theft and massacre. Plants and beasts devour each other in order to survive.

We are born only to serve as food for another. Despite the degree of civilization or, to phrase it better, perfectibility to which he has arrived, man is also subject to this law, and can escape it only under pain of death. He kills both plants and beasts to feed himself: he is insatiable.

Aside from the food that assures him life, man also nourishes himself on air, water, and light. But have we ever seen two men kill each other for the sharing of these aliments? Not that I know of. Nevertheless, these are the most precious of items, without which a man cannot live.

We can remain several days without absorbing the substances for which we make ourselves slaves. Can we do the same when it comes to air? Not even for a quarter of an hour. Water accounts for three-quarters of our organism and is indispensable in maintaining the elasticity of our tissues. Without heat, without the sun, life would be completely impossible.

And so, every man takes, steals his food. Do we accuse him of committing a crime? Of course not! Why then do we distinguish between food and everything else? Because everything else demands the expending of effort, a certain amount of labor. But labor is the very essence of society, that is, the association of all individuals to conquer with little effort much well-being. Is this truly the image of what exists? Are your institutions based on such a mode of organization? The truth demonstrates the contrary.

The more a man works the less he earns. The less he produces the more he benefits. Merit is not taken into consideration. Only the bold seize power and hasten to legalize their rapine.

From top to bottom of the social scale all is villainy on one side and idiocy on the other. Imbued with these truths, how can you expect that I could respect such a state of affairs?

A liquor seller and the boss of a brothel enrich themselves, while a man of genius dies of poverty in a hospital bed. The baker who bakes bread doesn't get any; the shoemaker who makes thousands of shoes shows his toes; the weaver who makes stocks of clothing doesn't have any to cover himself with; the bricklayer who builds castles and palaces wants for air in a filthy hovel. Those who produce everything have nothing, and those who produce nothing have everything.

Such a state of affairs can only produce antagonism between the laboring class and the owning—that is, the do-nothing—class. The fight breaks out, and hatred delivers its blows.

You call a man a thief and bandit; you apply the rigor of the law against him without asking yourself if he could be something else. Have we ever seen a *rentier* become a burglar? I admit that I've never heard of this. But I, who am neither a *rentier* nor a landlord, I, who am just a man who owns only his arms and his brains to ensure his preservation, had to conduct myself differently. Society only granted me three means of existence: work, begging, or theft. Work, far from being hateful, pleases me: man cannot do without working. His muscles and brain possess a sum of energy that must be spent. What I hated was sweating blood and tears for a pittance of a salary; it was creating wealth that wouldn't be allowed me.

In a word, I found it hateful to surrender to the prostitution of work. Begging is degradation, the negation of all dignity. Every man has a right to life's banquet.

The right to live isn't begged for, it's taken.

Theft is the restitution, the regaining of possession. Instead of being cloistered in a factory, like in a penal colony; instead of begging for what I had a right to, I preferred to rebel and fight my enemy face-to-face by making war on the rich, by attacking their property.

Of course, I understand that you would have preferred that I submit to your laws; that as a docile and worn-out worker I would have created wealth in exchange for a miserable salary, and when my body would have been worn out and my brain softened I would have died on a street corner. Then you wouldn't have called me a "cynical bandit," but an "honest worker." Employing flattery, you would even have given me the Medal of Labor. Priests promise paradise to their dupes. You are less abstract: you offer them a piece of paper.

I thank you for such goodness, such gratitude, messieurs. I'd prefer to be a cynic conscious of my rights rather than an automaton, a caryatid.

As soon as I achieved consciousness I engaged in theft without any scruples. I have no part in your so-called morality that advocates the respect of property as a virtue when in reality there are no worse thieves than landlords.

Consider yourselves lucky, messieurs, that this prejudice has taken root in the people, for this serves as your best gendarme. Knowing the powerlessness of the law or, to phrase it better, of force, you have made them your most solid protectors. But beware: everything only lasts a certain time. Everything that is constructed, built by trickery and force, can be demolished by trickery and force.

The people are evolving every day. Can't you see that having learned these truths, become conscious of their rights, all the starving, all the wretched, in a word, all your victims, are arming themselves with jimmies and assaulting your homes to take back the wealth they created and that you stole from them.

Do you think they'll be any unhappier? I think not. If they were to think carefully about this, they would prefer to run all possible risks rather than fatten you while groaning in misery.

"Prison … penal colonies … the gallows," it will be said. But what are these prospects in comparison with the life of a beast made up of all possible sufferings.

The miner who fights for his bread in the bowels of the earth, never seeing the sun shine, can perish from one minute to the next, victim of an explosion. The roofer who wanders across roofs can fall and be smashed to pieces. The sailor knows the day of his departure but doesn't know if he'll return to port. A good number of other workers contract fatal maladies in the exercise of their profession, wear themselves out, poison themselves, kill themselves to create for you, even gendarmes and policemen—your valets—who, for the bone you give them to nibble on, sometimes meet death in the fight they undertake against your enemies.

Stubbornly sticking to your narrow egoism, do you not remain skeptical regarding this vision? The people are frightened, you seem to be saying. We govern them through fear and repression. If a man cries out we'll throw him in prison; if he stumbles we'll deport him to the penal colony; if he acts we'll guillotine him! All of this is poorly calculated, messieurs, believe you me. The sentences you inflict are not a remedy for acts of revolt. Repression, far from being a remedy, or even a palliative, is only an aggravation of the evil.

Collective measures only sow hatred and vengeance. It's a fatal cycle. In any case, since the time you have been cutting off heads, since the time you have been filling the prisons and the penal colonies, have you prevented hatred from manifesting itself? Say something! Answer! The facts demonstrate your powerlessness.

For my part I knew full well that my conduct could have no other issue than the penal colony or the gallows. You certainly see that this did not prevent me from acting. If I engaged in theft it was not a question of gain, of lucre, but a question of principle, of right. I preferred to preserve my liberty, my independence, my dignity as a man rather than to make myself the artisan of someone else's fortune. To put it crudely, with no euphemisms: I preferred to rob rather than be robbed!

Of course, I too condemn the act through which a man violently and through ruse takes possession of the fruits of someone else's labor. But it's precisely because of this that I made war on the rich, the thieves of the goods of the poor. I too want to live in a society from which theft is banished. I only approved of and used theft as the means of revolt most appropriate for combating the most unjust of all thefts: individual property.

In order to destroy an effect you must first destroy the cause. If there is theft it is only because there is abundance on one hand and famine on the other; because *everything* only belongs to *some*. *The struggle will only disappear when men will place their joys and suffering in common, their labors and their riches, when all will belong to everyone.*

A revolutionary anarchist, I made my revolution. Vive l'anarchie!
For Germinal, to you, to the cause.

ANDRÉ LORULOT

André Lorulot, born in 1885, chose his pseudonym as an anagram of his actual name, Roulot. He was a controversial figure among individualists, not only because of his ideas but also because of the accusation that he was a police informant, one put forth in private by Victor Serge and in public by Jean Grave in his memoirs of anarchism (where he is simply named "L."). The charge of being an informant that haunted Lorulot was a common one in these circles, though, and the groundlessness of the charge is apparent both from his impeccable record as an activist and from the fact that the police monitored his activities for years.

Lorulot's first arrest for political activity occurred in 1905, when he jeered the king of Spain at a parade in Paris. That same year he helped Libertad found l'anarchie, *which he was to write for and then edit for the next six years. During that period, he also participated in an anarchist commune in the countryside, which, like all of its kind, collapsed within a couple of years as a result of internal dissension.*

He was again arrested in 1907 for "incitement of murder" and again the following year for encouraging soldiers to disobey orders.

After Libertad's death Lorulot assumed the leadership of l'anarchie from 1909 to 1911, where he focused on issues quite in the individualist mainstream, particularly scorn for unions and for government schools. He felt they did nothing but prepare future generations of keepers of order, and he called teachers "intellectual cops of the capitalist class."

As a result of disagreements with both the general line of l'anarchie, which was in his view far too supportive of illegalism, and with Victor Serge, who he felt gave too much weight to the sentiments, he left the paper in Serge's hands in mid-1911 and in December founded L'Idée Libre.

The sourness of Lorulot's relations with other anarchists became glaringly apparent in 1913 at the trial of the Bonnot Gang. As a witness, he was roughly handled by defendant Serge, then still known as Kibalchich, who confronted Lorulot about his opinions on illegalism (in 1906 Lorulot had written in defense of it). On the stand, Serge asked why Lorulot wasn't on trial for his opinions, though Serge was. In later correspondence with Émile Armand, Serge would further vent his spleen against Lorulot and refuse to work with any newspaper to which Lorulot was also a contributor.

*Ironically, like Serge, he would distance himself
from his anarchist individualist comrades at the time
of the Bolshevik Revolution, which he defended, including its handling of the Kronstadt rebellion and
the crushing of the anarchist Makhno guerrillas in
the Ukraine.*

*His final decades, though, were primarily dedicat-
ed to antireligious work, and at the time of his death
in 1963 he was president of the National Federation
of Free Thinkers.*

Who Are We? What Do We Want?

We don't have the pretension of responding in one article to questions as vast and interesting as these. This is the goal that our *Idée
Libre* proposes to fulfill, and we only want to indicate here an
overview of the work to be carried out, a work whose urgency and
necessity escape no one.

For too long we have contented ourselves with responding to
these questions with a few pompous clichés or sonorous phrases.
For too long we have limited ourselves to purely sentimental dec-
larations or virulent affirmations. We can't be satisfied with words
or dreams, and we think it is time to substitute precise concepts
based on discussion, experience, and knowledge for abstract formulas and puerile declamations.

Determining the rational and tangible goals of our activity
and envisaging the most serious and rapid means for realizing
them: this is the fruitful task we must seek to carry out. This is
the task that we want to collaborate in to the best of our ability.
Today in a few lines we are going to attempt to pose the question
on its true terrain while of course reserving the right to return
later to the different parts of the problem in order to debate them
more completely.

* * *

In the midst of the unspeakable chaos of philosophies of all kinds and of various moralities, we can cull the constant and persistent tendency that impels the *individual* toward life. Toward an ever-better life, freer and more noble: that is, toward happiness.

We are thus headed toward happiness, like all humans and all organized beings of whatever kind. The essential aspiration of every living being consists, in the first instance, in safeguarding one's own life and then improving it. Egoism? Instinct of preservation? Law of universal equilibrium? This is of no importance, and without quibbling over the interpretation of this fact we will limit ourselves to noting it.

And so we want to live. As long and as well as possible, and it will be easy for us to determine what this means. To be sure, men have never managed to come to an agreement on the meaning of the word "happiness." It is understood that this word expresses something variable, individual, impossible to fix in a collective and immutable ideal. But we have noted that everywhere and always the individual has sought happiness, so we don't have to concern ourselves with general or planetary happiness, but with our personal happiness. In any event, could we impose happiness on those who don't desire it or who see it in a different way than we do? Do we have the capacity to make our neighbor happy without his assistance? Not at all, and this is why the realization of happiness must above all be the work of the individual, and the fruit of his own efforts.

Far from us the pretension to want to dictate acts or present a new gospel. On the contrary, it is by the destruction of all credos, of all beliefs, that the individual can find the road to his happiness, to his life. But we say that the happiness of the individual can only consist in the rational flowering of his faculties, the free and conscious satisfaction of his needs, the preservation of his vitality, and the equilibrium of his functions. This is not a metaphysical definition that gives rise to interminable and sterile discussions. It rests on an experimental basis, easily controlled and of incontestable importance. Everything that is capable of atrophying one of my organs, one of my senses; everything that diminishes or can diminish my intelligence, my energy; everything that can trouble the functioning of my organism, dull my will, pervert my instincts, lead me to harmful acts, all of this is contrary to my life, contrary to my happiness, and, consequently, contrary to myself. "With all my might I will seek to cast aside these obstacles, to overcome these obstacles, to defend myself against aberrations, against absurd acts, for I want to realize my personality as fully as possible." This is what the reasoning individual will say in the face of life, after having swept the tables clean of all constraints.

Enemies of collective morality, of rules of conduct imposed on the individual, we want the latter to determine his morality for himself, freely, with no other guide than his own reason constantly enlightened by study and experience, as well as by his knowledge and his observations of his fellow men, controlled and verified by himself when this is needed.

Let us then repeat it: our work will consist in furnishing each individual with the elements that will permit him to establish his individual morality and to act as much as possible with the goal of conquering his happiness and improving his life. In our opinion this will be the best means for everyone to be able to usefully respond to the primordial questions that we often pose: "Who are we?" Men in love with burning, free, and conscious life. "What do we want?" To know the laws that preside over our existence in order to conduct ourselves both intensely and reasonably. An unlimited field of action is open before such efforts, capable of allowing us fertile results and radiant realizations.

* * *

Inevitably, putting such concepts into practice will lead us to engage in a struggle with social forces. It isn't enough to know where the good lies, it is necessary to want and to be able to conquer it. It isn't enough to know the value of one act or the absurdity of another, one must have the strength to effectuate the former and avoid the latter. The individual will thus be led to rebel against the institutions that want to maintain him in evil, against the men who do harm to his will, impose on him a form of life whose failings he recognizes. He becomes the adversary of all tyrannies, he rebels against all economic, material, and moral constraints. By reason of the numerous bonds that connect individual life to collective life, the individual cannot proclaim a lack of interest in the social question, since his personality will develop all the better if his ambient milieu is more propitious, more favorable, less authoritarian, constituted by men less closed-minded and more tolerant.

Nevertheless, before beginning the struggle it is good to know where you are going and what you want. Before acting, you must *know*. Let us thus learn.

Man will only be able to act usefully when he will have managed to destroy all lies, freed himself from all the superstitions error gives birth to, and sought the truth in the jumble of knowledge and observations. I will respond in the following way to those skeptics who will object that the truth doesn't exist: we call truth a controlled relationship among phenomena. These latter can vary, in the same way as the properties of bodies and the manifestations of beings, and in this case it is obvious that the truth transforms itself. We should thus not look on it as a dogma, but must seek it in all domains, without any preconceived spirit, relying on the exact data we possess. This will be its only true and solid foundation.

So, it is necessary for man to know his place in nature, and that he study the laws of universal evolution. He must give himself over to positive study, that is, study entirely based on facts, the phenomena he participates in, and the beings that surround him. This study can be both gradual and universal, should scrutinize every living being, every organ, every part of every animal and raise itself to the level of understanding the relations that connect the part to the whole, the cell to the body and the universe. Through the study of phenomena and the laws of instinct, the morality of animals, of their collective groupings, he will prepare himself to no be longer ignorant of the laws that guide the functioning of human reason, of psychological and social manifestations, of the evolution of the ideas and customs of our societies. By examining historical documents relating the efforts of those who preceded him, as well as through the knowledge of their labors and their ideas, he will find matter for fruitful reflections and profitable learning. When he will have acquired the knowledge that will permit him to consciously guide him, the individual will fortify himself through reflection and discussion, which will aid him in assimilating his intellectual nourishment in a more perfect way, and will develop his faculties of discernment and comprehension.

It goes without saying that we must not neglect physical culture and that all those sciences that are concerned with the maintenance of our health must be investigated. We want to live, that is, be able to ward off all that can degrade us, all forms of partial or total suicide, conscious or unconscious. The sciences dealing with general hygiene will teach us to search for the correct means of existence, to love pure air, the sun, cleanliness, healthy foods, rational exercise, healthy and agreeable lodgings. They will inspire hatred in us for slums, overwork, filth, ugliness, the hatred of artificial joys, of puerile vanity, of perversions that stupefy or taint. We will advance toward beauty, the reasonable and strong life, toward harmony and joy.

We must then develop our will so that it is able to assist our intelligence, which will have been enlightened. "To think and not act is the same as not thinking," one of our friends correctly said. We insist that education must be total, that it must develop all our faculties, all our senses. It doesn't consist in book learning alone, and whoever will be satisfied with retaining a few phrases and a certain number of poorly digested notions will not have brought together the conditions we have laid out, he will not know how to—will not be able to—properly conduct himself. The will requires educating, just like the intelligence, of which it is the auxiliary. We will exercise our will by casting aside those errors that can be dangerous, and we will maintain it through action, resistance to atavisms, the passions, to evil, by training it in the suppression of harmful acts, by the cultivation of daring, of initiative, of courage.

How unlimited is the horizon that opens up before the individual! He will be able to quench his thirst for knowledge, his desire for healthy joys without ever being afraid of tiring of them. Each of his efforts will bear within itself its reward by increasing his happiness, along with that of his kind.

For moral education is as necessary as purely intellectual education. As I said above, we cannot show interest in the lives of others, since our personal acts depend on those of other humans. This is where the error arises of those who use an extreme individualism to legitimize antisocial acts. After having established the rules for his conduct as concerns himself, the true individualist will concern himself with that part of morality that keeps in sight the relations of men among themselves. Not being able to ignore the benefits of solidarity and association, he will want to analyze the attitudes of his fellow men in order to draw the greatest profit, personal and durable, from mutual assistance. Through a prior selection and agreements based on affinities he will obtain the maximum amount of profit with the least concessions, and the happiness of the individual will thus be in harmony and equilibrium with that of his comrades.

Acting consciously toward himself and others: this is the goal that the man desirous of blossoming through reason and free agreement will propose for himself.

It is obvious that he must turn to those of his kind who are still in error, who accept their servitude. It will be in his interest to work for the emancipation of those capable of evolving and who can—after having escaped from ignorance—become fraternal and dedicated comrades, increasing the wealth and power of his life.

To be sure, the question will not be resolved by this summary exposé, nor do we have the naivete to believe this. We have simply attempted to indicate the overall picture of a flexible and individual morality based on liberty and reason. At the same time, we have outlined the plan for a colossal but marvelous labor. Is this not our entire task? Improve ourselves, reform ourselves, become more conscious, less flawed, less proud and impulsive and through our friendly criticism, our propaganda and comradely

efforts, strive to show the ignorant and the submissive the reno-
vating path of revolt and education.

We will here—and this will be the reason for this publica-
tion—study and determine the multiple rules of individual conduct. Stripped of all dogmatic spirit, but also of all mysticism
and skepticism, we will advance toward life with something other
than literary witticisms and sentimental impressions. Everything
capable of elevating man's mentality, everything that can assist
him in piercing nature's mysteries, in tasting science's teachings
universally applied, all of this will interest us. We want men who
know how to conduct themselves, who know what they are doing and what they want, and not chatterboxes, the regimented,
the infatuated, or vain and authoritarian fools. The task is difficult, but it is fascinating and fruitful! Accomplished methodically
and seriously it will be the true anarchist task, since it alone can
form better individuals, capable of living without authority, of
blossoming individually, and forever advancing toward the better
through honest solidarity. In the face of dogmas, of despots, of
the sentimental, of charlatans and regimenters, humanity's future
belongs to reason.

[From *L'Idee Libre*, no. 1, December 1911. After
a stormy period at *l'anarchie* Lorulot left the paper and started his own. This is the programmatic
statement that appeared in its first issue. —ed.]

Men Disgust Me

The Tyrant from Below
No, liberty is not for us. We
are too ignorant, too vain, too presumptuous,
too cowardly, too vile, too corrupted
—Marat

I have to say it and I will say it.

In taking up the pen I committed myself, all alone, to banishing all forms of partisanship and to refusing to retreat before any truths. Hypocrisy is repugnant to me, whether it's from the Right or the Left. This need for honesty has made me many enemies, even—and how ironic—among "friends" and "brothers."

Beat up on the capitalist and the fascist: that's fine. Bravo! You'll be encouraged, at least verbally (when you have to pay with your own money it's already more difficult—you end up paying with your skin).

But, honest man, don't allow yourself to criticize what is going on in your own house. Reveal the flaws of your neighbor but close your eyes to the turpitudes of your party.

I never knew how to do this. This is probably why I never wanted to join any party, any church, any sect. My independence is my most precious good.

This is not a comfortable position. You attract much animosity. The troublemaker. He who refuses to be the accomplice of the ambitious, the traitors, the profiteers. For they exist. And everywhere, everywhere.

I passionately love humanity and have dedicated my best efforts to the fight for the oppressed. All tyrants disgust me—along with all those who put up with them, adulate them, support them. After having brought them down will I make myself a tyrant in their place? I would be disgusted with myself.

People, beware of demagogues. They are your worst enemies. They caress you only so they can better shear you. Deep down they detest and mock you, but they need your shoulders to carry their kettledrum (which won't beat for you). They hate you, and if they could squeeze you once and for all in the vise they'd gladly do it. And perhaps later they will. For the moment they need your votes, your suffrage, and your dues. So they'll call you great, noble, and beautiful, and that you have both all rights and all virtues.

If you believe them you are an imbecile, and you are lost.

* * *

Telling a worker the truth, the whole truth, even when it is painful, is perhaps the best way of serving his cause and working for his true liberation.

They disgust me, those who tell the people they'll achieve complete and universal happiness without having to make an effort or perfecting themselves. They lie—and willfully. It is, incidentally, in their interest—that of the masters, or the aspiring masters—to prevent the masses from educating themselves. Is it not by correcting themselves that they will be capable of progressing and taking in hand the guiding of their own destiny? That day, having become useless, chiefs and leaders will have nothing to do but disappear.

They disgust me, those who refuse the worker the right to the ideal and speak exclusively of his belly.

For them, everything is subordinated to beefsteak.

An ever bigger, ever bloodier, ever easier-to-conquer beefsteak. The ideal of a wild beast, or a starving dog.

To be sure, one must live: I grant you this. But I add that we must live in order to develop in ourselves the highest and noblest qualities of man: Dignity! Consciousness! Love! Liberty!

What good would it be for me to gorge myself like a bulldog or to digest like a canon if I have to renounce the most elevated aspirations and the purest, most disinterested joys?

Don't listen to those who want to subordinate everything to the stomach: they insult you. Become capable of fighting for something other than tripe or the wallet. Without detesting them (let's not go from one extreme to the other), we should mistrust flatterers, professional politicians, phrasemakers. Let us go toward the truth, whatever it might be, with all our heart, without putting on blinders, without stifling anyone's voice.

I have no particular hatred for the rich. If it happens that I complain of their stupidity or mock their pretentions, I am not jealous of their money.

Must I add that it is not enough to be poor to earn my sympathy?

Money makes those who have it stupid or crooked. But those who don't have it are generally as cretinous and villainous as the rich. The desire to enrich themselves suffices to stifle in them all generous feelings and any aspiration to justice—and cleanliness.

And those 100 percent revolutionaries, those organized proletarians, those conscious union members, those pioneers of the
future who get as drunk as skunks? Who don't have ten francs
to buy a book but who spend twice that at the bar? Who stum-
ble around the streets and disgorge their wine while climbing
the stairs? Are these the pioneers of the future, the precursors of
the Harmonious City, with their dirty feet, their bestial ignorance, their animalistic pretentions, their appetite for alcohol and
bordellos?

* * *

Thanks to a certain minister named Pomaret, since last winter
workers who have been employed for sixty consecutive years in
the same establishment receive a medal of honor for labor.

You read correctly: they will give a medal to workers who have
remained sixty years with the same boss.

It's hard to more blatantly mock these poor proles.

But they accept the medal (which won't even be of chocolate). They will be as proud as peacocks and will strive to hold
upright their carcasses that have been emptied, worn out, crushed
by so much suffering, so much prolonged effort, so much pitiless
exploitation.

They'll be photographed with their little bauble. As proud,
as foolish as those fathers of fourteen whose unintelligent mugs
[the Catholic newspaper] La Croix (edited by bachelors) regularly
publishes.

The lowest of slaves is he who is happy to be one.

So admit it: in many ways the slave is as repugnant as his master.

If he trembles in a cowardly way before his superior, he aveng-
es himself in a no less cowardly way on his inferior.

A prole who stammers with servility before his factory foreman makes up for it in the evening by beating his wife and kids.
Then he stands up straight. And he shouts. Then he's a real male!

At the factory itself, if he has any apprentices under him he
uses them as whipping boys; he tyrannizes over them, wears them
out through ill treatment.

Just like the sergeant who works over the recruit at the barracks because the captain yelled at him.

Humanity doesn't shine too brightly.

* * *

Once we said: the people. Today we say: the masses.

Once we said: your delegates. Today there is the base and the summit.

The delegates, secretaries, and so on, we call them the *responsables*. Does that mean that the voters are all irresponsible? That is, unaware?

What contempt for the individual. Conformism is ever more triumphant. The human personality is neglected. What am I saying? It is disappearing. If it existed it would show itself, it would react, it would complain. It is only capable of bleating out applause and weakly following chiefs who lead it to the slaughterhouse. In the immense leveling of the social herds *Man* becomes increasingly rare. And we make life tougher and tougher for him.

With your millions of members, dues payers, you couldn't save the Spanish Republic. CGT, Communist and Socialist parties, what did you try that was effective? Seriously? All you know are materialistic demands, cash, but the Ideal, the defense of a great disinterested cause? How could your members know about this, since their bad shepherds never spoke to them about it?

The Imbecilic Crowd

I blush with shame when I think that I'm part of the imbecilic crowd that is shamelessly called "civilized peoples."

The whole world was shaken up by a sensational event: a Negro boxer beat a German boxer.

The bout took place in New York and was an unquestionable success: there were eighty thousand spectators. The box office was $1,000,000, about 35,000,000 French francs (which means the average price of a seat was 400 francs per person).

If you would have asked these people for 100 sous for some useful or fraternal work they would have sent you packing, saying they didn't have a penny and going on and on about how hard the times are, the crisis, the high cost of living, and the weight of taxes.

But as soon as it's a question of going to contemplate a black brute punching an Aryan brute on the chin, everyone rushes there, pushing the others out of the way.

People rush to Auteuil and Tremblay to see five or six nags run, ridden by clownish jockeys who are more or less in cahoots in swindling the imbecilic bettors.

When the young Cécile Sorel made her debut at the music hall, the Rue de Clichy was invaded by an enormous crowd. Englishmen came over by plane. Seats were scalped at 600 francs each.

At Juan-les-Pins people paid 100 francs to hear Cretino Rossi![1] Fights broke out among those in line so people could get in first. People pushed each other, they grumbled, they shook with anguish. And these people would have refused to make the least effort for something useful or healthy.

People push and shove at the bullfight of death. Ten or twenty pesetas for a ticket. Twenty thousand spectators, men and women, bray and shout, inciting the matador with gestures and words. What a treat it is to enjoy the sufferings of a wheezy horse paralyzed with fear, whose intestines are wrapped around the bull's horns!

And the sadists who revel in cock fights.

And the sick people who give 500 francs to the madam in order to have the right to apply the whip to the more or less saggy posterior of a whore, who will receive only 50 for her degradation.

Man is terribly fond of gawking, terribly sheeplike.

His civilized varnish is superficial, and he easily allows himself to be dragged along by the whims of fashion, unthinking enthusiasms, the tutelage of what-will-the-neighbors-think, and the cruel and bloody intoxication of unbridled crowds.

Tell me about it at the next war to end all wars!

On the Boulevard Barbès, near the metro, a man comes running out of a restaurant.

---

1   The popular singer Tino Rossi. —ed.

Immediately a murmur rises above the strolling crowd. Fifty, a hundred people start running. And soon there's an immense multitude that's running after the fleeing man, his features livid and contracted, as he runs straight ahead to escape the pack.

What did he do? What became of him? I never knew. But I was almost torn to pieces right there, for having uttered some reflections out loud about the cowardice and stupidity of the people who shouted and struck without knowing why. What imprudence! I was shouted at and threatened. And by women! Young and perhaps pretty, if they hadn't been disfigured by anger.

Of course, their pimps were ready at their side. ... Contemptible crowd. How I despise you!

[From *Les Hommes me dégoutent*. [Herblay]:
L'Idée Libre, 1939.]

HAN RYNER

Born Henri Ner in 1861, he joined the Freemasons while still young and first achieved notoriety in 1892 when he advocated the socialization of bread, a campaign that, though never implemented, achieved no small amount of attention. By 1898 he had assumed the name Han Ryner and published a novel whose title can serve as the program of anarchist individualism: The Crime of Obeying. *He preached a gentle variety of individualism, one more inspired by Epicurus than Stirner, and though his writings were disdained by the more militant individualists, he was much admired and in demand. He taught individualism and anarchism at the Université Populaire and was particularly close to the eclectic Émile Armand, writing for several of the latter's papers, as well as* L'Idée Libre *of André Lorulot. World War I inspired him to prioritize antimilitarism and antipatriotism. He actively defended political victims of the war—draft dodgers and soldiers convicted of insubordination—and testified in support of conscientious objectors before military tribunals. He despised any separations, either class or national, between peoples.*

> *He died in 1938, still fighting against colonial-*
> *ism, still supporting the establishing of anarchist col-*
> *onies in the countryside, and still battling the church.*

Antipatriotism

Will I manage to avoid here those considerations that belong more in the articles on "Fatherland" and "Patriotism"?

From the moment patriotism reigned, antipatriotism was the reaction of reason and sentiment. It assumed diverse forms in accordance with the degree to which it relied more or less consciously on individualism, on love for all men, on love for one man (as with Camilla, the sister of the Horatii), or even on a reasoned or sentimental preference for the laws and morals of a foreign country.

Buddha was necessarily hostile to any patriotic exclusivism, this man who doesn't even admit what can be called human chauvinism, extending his loving mercy to all living beings. In Greece the Sophists were antipatriotic. Socrates, the greatest of them, proclaimed: "I am not Athenian; I am a citizen of the world." He condemned the fatherland in the name of "unwritten laws," that is, in the name of conscience. Other Sophists rejected it in the name of a more interested individualism. Nevertheless, their contemporary Aristophanes detested his democratic fatherland because he admired the aristocratic organization of Lacedemonia. (Thus Mr. Paul Bourget and Mr. Léon Daudet, dazzled by the power of the German command had their years of naive patriotism: little gigolos who almost inevitably surrender themselves to the most fearsome "terror.") Plato and Xenophon, poor disciples of Socrates who falsify and use him a bit like Mr. Charles Maurras falsifies and uses Mr. Auguste Comte, have sentiments similar to those of Aristophanes. Xenophon ended by fighting against his fatherland in the ranks of the Lacedemonians.

The Cyrenaic philosophers were antipatriotic. One of them, Theodore the Atheist, repeated the line of many wise men: "The world is my fatherland." He added, "Sacrificing oneself to the fatherland means renouncing wisdom in order to save the mad." In which he is wrong: it means assisting the mad in destroying themselves.

The Cynics boldly professed antipatriotism. Antisthenes mocks those who are proud of being autochtonous, a glory they share—he notes—with a certain number of slugs and marvelous grasshoppers. Diogenes, in order to make fun of the emotional activities of patriots, rolled his barrel across a besieged city. His disciple, the Cretan Krates, declared: "I am a citizen not of Thebes, but of Diogenes."

Plutarch reproaches the Epicureans and Stoics for the disdainful practical antipatriotism that kept them from all public employment. The Epicurean only admitted select sentiments and gave his heart to only a few friends, who might be from any country. The Stoic extended his love to all men. He obeyed "the nature that made man the friend of man, not from interest, but from the heart." Four centuries before Christianity he invented charity, which unites all those who participate in reason, both men and gods, in one family.

The first Christians were as antipatriotic as the Stoics, the Epicureans, and the other sages. Those of Judea were not moved by the ruin of Jerusalem. Those from Rome stubbornly predicted the fall of Rome. They only loved the celestial fatherland, and Tertullian said in their name: "The thing that is most foreign to us is the public sphere." They were faithful to the spirit of the gospel, where a certain parable of the Good Samaritan would be translated by a truly Christian Frenchman into the parable of the good Prussian, though an evangelical German would turn it into the parable of the good Frenchman. And "good" wouldn't have the same meaning that it does for a Hindenburg or the academician Joffre. Catholicity means universality. Catholicism is international and consequently, if it is conscious and sincere, is a form of antipatriotism. A more recent International wants to replace war with revolution, and hostilities between nations with the class struggle. The principles of Catholicism don't allow a distinction between the faithful and the nonbelievers. Modern Catholics boast of their patriotism without realizing that this means denying their catholicity. Thus the members of the Socialist or Communist parties who consent to "national defense" would, knowingly or not, cease to be able to call themselves socialists. The Catholic meaning still lives in a few men, in Gustave Dupin, author of *La Guerre Infernale*, in Grillot de Givry, author of *Le Christ et la Patrie*, in Dr. Henri Mariave, author of *La Philosophie Suprême*. They are thus considered an abomination by their so-called brothers.

The antipatriotic truth was never explained by anyone with more balanced force and clear consciousness than by Tolstoy. His pamphlet "Patriotism and the Government" shows to what extent "patriotism is a backward idea, inopportune and harmful. … As a sentiment patriotism is an evil and harmful sentiment; as a doctrine it is nonsensical, since it is clear that if every people and every state takes itself for the best of peoples and states then they have all made an outlandish and harmful mistake." He then explains how "this ancient idea, though in flagrant contradiction with the entire order of things, which has changed in other aspects, continues to influence men and guide their acts." Only those in power, using the easily hypnotizable foolishness of the people, find it "advantageous to maintain this idea, which no longer has any meaning or usefulness." They succeed in this because they own the sold-out press, the servile university, the brutal army, the corrupting budget, "the most powerful means for influencing men."

Except when it's a question of demands by natives of the colonies, or the separatist sentiments of a few Irishmen, a few Bretons, or a few Occitanians, the word patriotism is almost always used today in a lying fashion. The sacrifices demanded "for the fatherland" are in reality offered to another divinity, to the nation that destroyed and robbed our fatherland, whichever it might be. No one any longer has a fatherland in the large and heterogeneous modern nations. …

If it remains exclusive, the love for the land of our birth is foolish, absurd, and the enemy of progress. If it were to become a means of intelligence, I would praise it in the same way that the man who rests in the shade of a tree praises the seed. From my love for the land of my childhood and for the language that, I might say, first smiled on my ears, comes love for the beauties of all of nature and the pensive music of all human languages. May my pride in my mountain teach me to admire other summits; may the gentleness of my river teach me to commune with the dream of all waters; from the charm of my forest, may I learn to find it in the measured grace of all woods; may the love of a known idea never turn me from a new idea or an enrichment that comes from afar. In the same way that a man grows beyond the size of a child, the first beauties we meet serve to have us ideally understand, taste, and conquer all beauties. What poverty to hear in these naive memories a poor and moving language that prevents our hearing other languages! From among our childhood memories let us love the alphabet that allows us to read all the texts offered by the successive or simultaneous riches of our life.

[From *L'Encyclopèdie Anarchiste*. Paris: Librairie Internationale, 1934.]

Mini-Manual of Individualism

I have adopted here the question-and-answer format, so handy for rapid exposition. In this case it is not the expression of any dogmatic pretensions: one won't find here a master who interrogates and a disciple who responds. There is, instead, an individualist questioning himself. In the first line I wanted to indicate that this was an interior dialogue. While the catechism asks: "Are you Christian?" I ask: "Am I individualist?" However, if it were prolonged, this procedure would bring with it some inconvenience and, having laid out my intention, I remembered that the soliloquy often employs the second person.

Brought together in this book are truths that are certain but whose certainty can only be discovered within oneself, along with opinions that are probable. There are problems that admit of several responses. Others—aside from the heroic solution, which can be advised only when all else is crime—lack an entirely satisfactory solution, and the approximations I propose are not superior to other approximations: I don't insist on mine. A reader who is incapable of setting out and, of acquiescing to truths, of finding probabilities analogous to my probabilities and in many cases more harmonious with himself, would not be worthy of the name of individualist.

Due to lack of development, or for other reasons, I will often leave even the most fraternal of spirits unsatisfied. I can only recommend to men of goodwill a careful reading of Epictetus's *Manual*. There, better than anywhere else, can be found the response to our worries and doubts. There, more than anywhere else, he who is capable of true courage will find the source of courage.

From Epictetus, as well as others, I have borrowed formulas without always thinking it necessary to indicate my debts. In a work like this one it is the things that matter, not their origin, and we eat more than one fruit without asking the gardener the name of the river or stream that fertilizes his garden.

Chapter I: On Individualism and a Few Individualists

Am I an individualist?

I am an individualist.

What do I mean by individualism?

I mean by individualism the moral doctrine that, relying on no dogma, no tradition, no external determination, appeals only to the individual conscience.

Hasn't the word "individualism" only designated this doctrine?

The name of individualism has often been given to the appearance of doctrines that are aimed at covering cowardly or conquering or aggressive egoism with a philosophical mask.

Cite a cowardly egoist who is sometimes called an individualist.

Montaigne.

Do you know of any conquering and aggressive egoists who proclaim themselves to be individualists?

All those who extend the brutal law of the struggle for life to relations between men.

Cite some names.

Stendhal, Nietzsche.

Name some true individualists.

Socrates, Epicurus, Jesus, Epictetus.

Why do you love Socrates?

He didn't teach a truth external to those who listened to him, but rather taught them to find the truth within themselves.

How did Socrates die?

He died condemned by laws and judges, assassinated by the city, a martyr to individualism.

What was he accused of?

Of not honoring the gods the city honored and of corrupting youth.

What did this last grievance mean?

It meant that Socrates professed opinions disagreeable to those in power.

Why do you love Epicurus?

Beneath his carefree elegance, he was a hero.

Cite a clever phrase of Seneca's concerning Epicurus.

Seneca calls Epicurus "a hero disguised as a woman."

What was the good that Epicurus did?

He delivered his disciples from the fear of gods or God, which is the beginning of madness.

What was Epicurus's great virtue?

Temperance. He distinguished between natural and imaginary needs. He showed that very little was needed to satisfy hunger and thirst, to defend oneself against heat and the cold. And he liberated himself from all other needs, that is, almost all the desires and all the fears that enslave men.

How did Epicurus die?

He died of a long and painful illness while boasting of a perfect happiness.

In general, do we know the true Epicurus?

No. Unfaithful disciples covered his doctrines with vice, in the same way a sore is hidden beneath a stolen coat.

Is Epicurus guilty of what false disciples have him say?

We are never guilty of the foolishness or perfidy of others.

Is the perversion of Epicurus's doctrine an exceptional phenomenon?

> Every word of truth, if it is listened to by many men, is transformed into a lie by the superficial, the crafty, and charlatans.

Why do you love Jesus?

> He lived free and a wanderer, a stranger to any social ties. He was the enemy of priests, external cults, and, in general, all organizations.

How did he die?

> Pursued by priests, abandoned by judicial authority, he died nailed to the cross by soldiers. Along with Socrates, he is the most celebrated victim of religion, the most illustrious martyr to individualism.

In general, do we know the real Jesus?

> No. The priests crucified his doctrine as well as his body. They transformed the tonic beverage into a poison. On the falsified words of the enemy of external organizations and cults they founded the most organized and most pompously empty of religions.

Is Jesus guilty of what disciples and priests have made of his doctrine?

> We are never guilty of the foolishness or perfidy of others.

Why do you love Epictetus?

The Stoic Epictetus courageously bore poverty and slavery. He was perfectly happy in the situations most painful to ordinary men.

How do we know Epictetus's doctrine?

His disciple Arrien gathered together some of his sayings in a small book entitled *The Manual of Epictetus*.

What do you think of *The Manual of Epictetus*?

Its precise and unfailing nobility, its simplicity free of any charlatanism renders it more precious to me than the Gospels. Epictetus's *Manual* is the most beautiful and liberating of all books.

In history are there not other celebrated individualists?

There are others. But those I have named are the purest and the easiest to understand.

Why do you not name the Cynics Antisthenes and Diogenes?

Because the Cynic doctrine is but a draft outline of Stoicism.

Why do you not name Xenon of Citium, the founder of Stoicism?

His life was admirable and, according to the testimony of the ancients, always resembled his philosophy. But today he is less well-known than those I have named.

Why do you not name the Stoic Marcus Aurelius?

Because he was an emperor.

Why do you not name Descartes?

Descartes was an intellectual individualist. He wasn't a clearly moral individualist. His actual morality appears to have been Stoic, but he didn't dare make it public. He only made known a "provisional morality" in which he recommends obeying the laws and customs of your country, which is the contrary of individualism. What is more, he seems to have lacked philosophical courage in other circumstances.

Why do you not name Spinoza?

Spinoza's life was admirable. He lived modestly, on a few grains of groats and a bit of milk soup. Refusing the pulpits that were offered him, he always earned his daily bread through manual labor. His moral doctrine is a stoic mysticism. But too exclusively intellectual, he professed a strange absolutist politics and, in the face of power, only maintained the freedom to think. In any case, his name puts one in mind more of a great metaphysical power than of a great moral beauty.

Chapter II: Preparation for Practical Individualism

Is it enough to proclaim oneself individualist?

No. A religion can be satisfied with verbal adherence and a few acts of adoration. A practical philosophy that isn't practiced is nothing.

Why can religions show more indulgence than moral doctrines?

The gods of religions are mighty monarchs. They save the faithful through grace and miracles. They grant salvation in exchange for the Law, certain ritual words and certain agreed-upon acts. They can even give me credit for acts done and words spoken for me by mercenaries.

What must I do to truly deserve the name of individualist?

All my acts must be in agreement with my ideas.

Is that agreement not difficult to obtain?

It is less difficult than it seems.

Why?

The beginning individualist is held back by false goods and bad habits. He only liberates himself at the cost of some effort. But the discord between his acts and his ideas is more painful to him than all renunciations. He suffers from it in the same way that a musician suffers from lack of harmony. At no price would the musician want to pass his life amid discordant noises. In the same way my lack of harmony is, for me, the greatest of sufferings.

What do we call the effort of putting one's life in agreement with one's thoughts?

It is called virtue.

Does virtue receive a reward?

Virtue is its own reward.

What do these words mean?

They mean two things: (1) If I think of a reward I am not virtuous. Disinterestedness is the primary characteristic of virtue. (2) Disinterested virtue creates happiness.

What is happiness?

> Happiness is the state of the soul that feels itself free of all outside servitudes and feels itself in perfect accord with itself.

Is it not then the case that there is only happiness when there is no longer a need to make an effort, and does happiness succeed virtue?

> The wise man always needs effort and virtue. He is always attacked from without. But, in fact, happiness only exists in a soul where there is no longer internal struggle.

Are we unhappy in pursuit of wisdom?

> No. While awaiting happiness each victory produces joy.

What is joy?

> Joy is the feeling of passing from a lesser to a greater perfection. Joy is the feeling that we are advancing toward happiness.

Distinguish between joy and happiness by a comparison.

> A peaceful being, forced to fight, carries off a victory that brings him nearer to peace: he feels joy. He finally arrives at a peace that nothing can trouble: he has reached happiness.

Should one attempt to obtain happiness and perfection the first day we understand them?

> It is rare that we can attempt immediate perfection without imprudence.

What dangers do the imprudent risk?

> The danger of retreating and becoming discouraged.

What is the right way to prepare oneself for perfection?

> It is right to go to Epictetus by passing through Epicurus.

What do you mean?

> One must first place oneself from the point of view of Epicurus and distinguish natural from imaginary needs. When we are able to despise in practice all that is unnecessary to life, when we disdain luxury and comfort, when we savor the physical pleasure that comes from simple food and drink, when our bodies as well as our souls will know the goodness of bread and water, then we will be able to advance further along the road.

What steps remain to be taken?

> It remains to be felt that even if deprived of bread and water we could be happy; that in the most painful illness, where we have no assistance, we could be happy; that even dying under torture in the midst of the insults of the crowd we could be happy.

Are these peaks of wisdom reachable by all?

> These peaks are reachable by all men of goodwill who feel a natural penchant toward individualism.

What is the intellectual path that leads to these peaks?

> It is the Stoic doctrine of the true good and the true evil.

What do we call this doctrine again?

> We call this the doctrine of things that depend on us and those that don't depend on us.

What are the things that depend on us?

> Our opinions, our desires, our inclinations, and our aversions: in a word, all our internal acts.

What are the things that don't depend on us?

> The body, riches, reputation, dignities: in a word, all those things that are not counted among our internal acts.

What are the characteristics of the things that depend on us?

> They are free by nature: nothing can stop them or place an obstacle before them.

What is the other name of the things that don't depend on us?

> The things that don't depend on us are also called indifferent things.

Why?

> Because none of them is either a true good or a true evil.

What happens to he who takes indifferent things for things that are good or evil?

> He finds obstacles everywhere. He is afflicted, he is troubled; he complains of things and of men.

Does he not feel an even greater evil?

He is a slave to desire and fear.

What is the state of a man who knows in practice that the things that don't depend on us are a matter of indifference?

He is free. No one can force him to do what he doesn't want to do or prevent him from doing what he wants to do. He has nothing to complain about of any thing or person.

Illness, prison, and poverty, for example: don't they diminish my liberty?

External things can diminish the liberty of my body and my movements. They aren't hindrances to my will as long as I don't suffer from the folly of desiring that which doesn't depend on me.

Doesn't the doctrine of Epicurus suffice during the course of life?

Epicurus's doctrine suffices if I have the things necessary for life and if my health is good. In the face of joy it renders me the equal of animals, who don't forge for themselves imaginary worries and ills. But in illness and hunger it no longer suffices.

Does it suffice in social relations?

In the course of social relations it can suffice. It liberated me from all the tyrants who have power over only the superfluous.

Are there social circumstances where it no longer suffices?

It no longer suffices if the tyrant can deprive me of bread, if he can put me to death or wound my body.

Who do you call a tyrant?

> I call a tyrant whoever, in acting on indifferent things—
> such as my wealth or body—claims to act on my will. I call
> a tyrant whoever attempts to modify my mood by means
> other than reasonable persuasion.

Are there not individualists for whom Epicureanism suffices?

> Whatever my present might be, I am ignorant of the fu-
> ture. I don't know if the great attack, where Epicureanism
> will no longer suffice, is lying in wait for me. I must
> then, as soon as I have attained Epicurean wisdom, work
> at continually strengthening myself until I reach Stoic
> invulnerability.

How will I live in calm?

> In calm I can live gently and temperately like Epicurus,
> but with the spirit of Epictetus.

In order to attain perfection, is it useful to propose for oneself
a model like Socrates, Jesus, or Epictetus?

> This is a bad method.

Why?

> Because it is my harmony I must realize, not that
> of another.

What kinds of obligations are there?

> There are two kinds of obligations: universal and per-
> sonal obligations.

What do you call universal obligations?

I call universal obligations those incumbent on
any wise man.

What do you call personal obligations?

I call personal obligations those that are incumbent on
me in particular.

Do personal obligations exist?

Personal obligations exist. I am a particular being who
finds himself in particular situations. I have a certain
degree of physical strength, of intellectual strength, and I
possess greater or lesser wealth. I have a past to continue.
I have to fight against a hostile destiny or collaborate in a
friendly one.

Distinguish in a simple way between personal and universal
obligations.

Without any exception, universal obligations are
obligations of abstention. Almost all obligations of action
are personal obligations. Even in those rare circumstances
where action is imposed on all, the detail of the act will
bear the mark of the agent, will be like the signature of the
moral artist.

Can personal obligation contradict universal obligation?

No. It is like the flower that can only grow on the plant.

Are my personal obligations the same as those of Socrates,
Jesus, or Epictetus?

They don't resemble them at all if I don't lead an apos-
tolic life.

Who will teach me my personal and universal obligations?

My conscience.

How will it teach me my universal obligations?

By telling me what I can expect from every wise man.

How will it teach me my personal obligations?

By telling me what I should demand of myself.

Are there difficult obligations?

There are no difficult obligations for the wise man.

Can the ideas of Socrates, Jesus, and Epictetus be useful to me when facing difficulty before I attain wisdom?

They can be useful to me, but I would never portray these great individualists as models.

How do I portray them?

I portray them as witnesses. And I want them never to condemn my way of acting.

Are these serious and slight errors?

Any error recognized as such before being committed is serious.

Theoretically, in order to judge my situation or that of others on the path to wisdom, can I not differentiate between serious and slight errors?

I can.

What do I call a slight error?

> I ordinarily call a slight error one that Epictetus would condemn and Epicurus wouldn't condemn.

What do I call a serious error?

> I call a serious error one that would be condemned even by the indulgence of Epicurus.

Chapter III: On the Mutual Relations between Individuals

Explain the formula defining obligations toward others.

> You will love your neighbor like yourself and your god above all.

Who is my neighbor?

> Other men.

Why do you call other men your neighbor?

> Because, gifted with reason and will, they are closer to me than are animals.

What do animals have in common with me?

> Life, feelings, intelligence.

Don't these common characteristics create obligations toward animals?

> These common characteristics create in me the obligation to not make animals suffer, to avoid causing them useless suffering, and to not kill them unnecessarily.

What right is given me by the absence of reason and will in animals?

> Animals not being persons; I have the right to make use of them in keeping with their strength and to transform them into instruments.

Do I have the same right over certain men?

> I never have the right to consider a man as a means. Every person is a goal, an end. I can only ask people for services that they will freely grant me, either through benevolence or in exchange for other services.

Are there not inferior races?

> There are no inferior races. The noble individual can flourish in all races.

Are there not inferior individuals incapable of reason and will?

> With the exception of the madman, every man is capable of reason and will. But many only listen to their passions and only have whims. It is among them that we meet those who have the pretension to command.

Can't I make instruments of incomplete individuals?

> No. I must consider them as individuals whose development has been halted, but in whom the man will perhaps be awakened tomorrow.

What am I to think of the orders of those with the pretension of commanding?

> An order can only ever be the caprice of a child or the fantasy of a madman.

How should I love my neighbor?

Like myself.

What do these words mean?

They mean: in the same way that I should love myself.

Who will teach me how I should love myself?

The second part of the formula teaches me how I should love myself.

Repeat that second part.

You will love your god above all else.

What is god?

God has several meanings: he has a different meaning in every religion or metaphysic, and he has a moral meaning.

What is the moral meaning of the word "god"?

God is the name of moral perfection.

What does the possessive "your" mean in the formula for love: "You will love *your* god"?

My god is my moral perfection.

What must I love above all else?

My reason, my freedom, my internal harmony, and my happiness, for these are the other names of my god.

Does my god demand sacrifices?

My god demands that I sacrifice my desires and my fears. He demands that I detest false goods and that I be "poor in spirit."

What else does he demand?

He also demands that I be ready to sacrifice to him my sensibility and, if need be, my life.

What then will I love in my neighbor?

I have the same obligations toward the sensibilities of my neighbor as I do toward the sensibilities of animals or myself.

Explain yourself.

I will not create pointless suffering in others or myself.

Can I create pointless suffering?

I cannot actively create pointless suffering. But certain necessary abstentions will result in suffering in others or myself. I should no more sacrifice my god to the sensibility of others than to my sensibility.

What are my obligations toward the lives of others?

I must neither kill nor injure them.

Are there not cases where we have the right to kill?

In the case of self-defense it would seem that necessity creates the right to kill. But in almost all cases, if I am brave enough, I will maintain the calm that permits us to save ourselves without killing.

Is it not better to be attacked without defending oneself?

> In this case abstention is, in fact, the sign of a superior virtue, the truly heroic solution.

In the face of the suffering of others, are there not unjustified abstentions that are exactly equivalent to evil acts?

> There are. If I allow a man to die whom I could have saved without crime, I am a veritable assassin.

Cite a phrase of Bossuet's dealing with this.

> "This rich inhuman being has stripped the poor man because he did not clothe him. He cruelly murdered him because he did not feed him."

What do you think of sincerity?

> Sincerity is my primary obligation toward others and myself, the testimony that my god demands as a continual sacrifice, like a flame that I must never allow to be extinguished.

What is the most necessary sincerity?

> The proclamation of my moral certainties.

What sincerity do you put in second place?

> Sincerity in the expression of my sentiments.

Is exactitude in the exposition of external facts without importance?

It is much less important than the two great philosophical and sentimental sincerities. Nevertheless, the wise man observes it.

How many kinds of lies are there?

There are three kinds of lies: the malicious lie, the officious lie, and the joyful lie.

What is a malicious lie?

The malicious lie is a crime and an act of cowardice.

What is an officious lie?

An officious lie is one that has usefulness to others or myself as its goal.

What do you think of the officious lie?

When an officious lie contains no harmful element, the wise man doesn't condemn it in others, but he avoids it himself.

Are there not cases where the officious lie is needed; if a lie can, for example, save someone's life?

In this case the wise man can tell a lie that doesn't touch on the facts. But he will almost always, instead of lying, refuse to respond.

Is a joyful lie permitted?

The wise man forbids himself the joyful lie.

Why?

The joyful lie sacrifices to a game the authority of words that, when maintained, can sometimes be useful to others.

Does the wise man forbid himself fiction?

The wise man doesn't forbid himself any open fiction, and it happens that he recounts parables, fables, symbols, and myths.

What should the relations between men and women be?

The relations between a man and a woman should be, like all relations between people, absolutely free on both sides.

Are there rules to be observed in these relations?

They should express mutual sincerity.

What do you think of love?

Mutual love is the most beautiful of indifferent things, the nearest to being a virtue. It makes a kiss noble.

Is a kiss without love a fault?

If a kiss without love is the meeting of two desires and two pleasures, it doesn't constitute a fault.

Chapter IV: On Society

Do I not have relations with isolated individuals?

I have relations, not only with isolated individuals, but also with various social groups and, in general, with society.

What is society?

Society is a gathering of individuals for a common labor.

Can a common labor be good?

Under certain conditions a common labor can be good.

Under what conditions?

A common labor will be good if, through mutual love or through love of the task, workers all act freely, and if their common efforts bring them together in a harmonious coordination.

Does social labor in fact have this characteristic of liberty?

In fact, social labor has no characteristics of liberty. Workers are subordinated to each other. Their efforts are not spontaneous and harmonious acts of love but grinding acts of constraint.

What do you conclude from this characteristic of social labor?

I conclude from this that social labor is evil.

How does the wise man consider society?

The wise man considers society as a limit. He feels social in the same way he feels mortal.

What is the attitude of the wise man in face of these limits?

The wise man regards these limits as material necessities, and he physically submits to them with indifference.

What are limits for one on the march toward wisdom?

> Limits constitute dangers for one on the march toward wisdom.

Why?

> He who cannot yet distinguish in practice, with unshakable certainty, between the things that depend on him and those that are indifferent, risks translating material constraints into moral constraints.

What should the imperfect individualist do in the face of social constraints?

> He should defend his reason and his will against them. He will reject the prejudices it imposes on other men, and he will forbid himself from hating or loving it. He will progressively free himself from any fear or desire concerning it. He will advance toward perfect indifference, which is what wisdom is when confronting things that do not depend on him.

Does the wise man hope for a better society?

> The wise man forbids himself any hope.

Does the wise man believe in progress?

> He notes that wise men are rare in all eras and that there is no moral progress.

Does the wise man take joy in material progress?

> The wise man notes that material progress has as its object the increasing of the artificial needs of some and the labor of others. Material progress appears to him to be an

increasing weight, which increasingly plunges man in the mud and in suffering.

Won't the invention of perfected machines diminish human labor?

The invention of machines has always aggravated labor. It has rendered it more painful and less harmonious. It has replaced free and intelligent initiative with a servile and fearful precision. It has made of the laborer, once the smiling master of tools, the trembling slave of the machine.

How can the machine, which multiplies products, not diminish the quantity of labor to be furnished by man?

Man is greedy, and the folly of imaginary needs grows as it is satisfied. The more superfluous things the madman has, the more he wants.

Does the wise man carry out social acts?

The wise man notes that in order to carry out social acts one must act on crowds, and one doesn't act on crowds through reason, but through the passions. He doesn't believe that he has the right to stir up the passions of men. Social action appears to him to be a tyranny, and he abstains from taking part in this.

Is the wise man not selfish in forgetting the happiness of the people?

The wise man knows that the words "the happiness of the people" have no meaning. Happiness is internal and individual. It can only be produced within oneself.

Does the wise man then have no pity for the oppressed?

The wise man knows that the oppressed who complain aspire to be oppressors. He relieves them according to his means, but he doesn't believe in salvation through common action.

The wise man then doesn't believe in reform?

He notes that reforms change the names of things and not the things themselves. The slave became a serf, and then a salaried worker: nothing has been reformed but language. The wise man remains indifferent to these questions of philology.

Is the wise man revolutionary?

Experience proves to the wise man that revolutions never have lasting results. Reason tells him that lies are not refuted by lies, and that violence isn't destroyed by violence.

What does the wise man think of anarchy?

The wise man regards anarchy as a form of naivete.

Why?

The anarchist believes that the government is the limit of liberty. He hopes, by destroying government, to expand liberty.

Is he not right?

The true limit is not government, but society. Government is a social product like any other. We don't destroy a tree by cutting one of its branches.

Why does the wise man not work at destroying society?

Society is as inevitable as death. On a material level our strength is weak against such limits. But the wise man destroys in himself the fear of society, just as he destroys the fear of death. He is indifferent to the political and social form of the milieu in which he lives, just as he is indifferent to the kind of death that awaits him.

So the wise man will never act on society?

The wise man knows that we can destroy neither social injustice nor the waters of the sea. But he strives to save an oppressed person from a particular injustice, just as he throws himself into the water to save a drowning man.

Chapter V: On Social Relations

Is work a social or a natural law?

Work is a natural law made worse by society.

How does society worsen the natural law of work?

In three ways: (1) It arbitrarily dispenses a certain number of men from all work and places their portion of the burden on other men. (2) It employs many men at useless labors and social functions. (3) It multiplies among all, and particularly among the rich, imaginary needs, and it imposes on the poor the odious labor necessary for the satisfaction of these needs.

Why do you find the law of work natural?

Because my body has natural needs that can only be satisfied by products of labor.

So, you only consider manual labor to be labor?

Without a doubt.

Doesn't the spirit also have natural needs?

Exercise is the only natural need of our intellectual faculties. The spirit forever remains a happy child who needs movement and play.

Aren't special workers needed to give the spirit occasions for play?

The spectacle of nature, the observation of human passions, and the pleasure of conversation suffice for the natural needs of the spirit.

So, you condemn art, science, and philosophy?

I don't condemn these pleasures. Like love, they are noble as long as they remain disinterested. In art, in science, in philosophy, in love, the delight I feel in giving to myself shouldn't be paid for by he who enjoys the delight in receiving.

But there aren't there artists who create with pain and scholars who seek with fatigue?

If the pain is greater than the pleasure, I don't understand why these poor people don't abstain.

So, you would demand manual labor of the artist and the scholar?

As is the case with lovers, nature demands manual labor of the scholar and artist since it imposes natural needs on them, as on other men.

The infirm also have material needs, and you wouldn't be so cruel as to impose a task on them they wouldn't be capable of?

Without a doubt, but I don't consider the beauty of a body or the force of a mind to be infirmities.

So, the individualist will work with his hands?

Yes, as much as possible.

Why do you say, "as much as possible"?

Because society has rendered obedience to natural law difficult. There is not remunerative manual labor for all. Ordinarily, we awaken to individualism too late to do an apprenticeship in a manual trade. Society has stolen from all in order to turn over to a few that great instrument of natural labor, the earth.

The individualist then can, in the current state of things, live off a task that he doesn't consider true labor?

He can.

Can the individualist be a functionary?

Yes, but he can't agree to all kinds of functions.

What are the functions the individualist will abstain from?

The individualist will abstain from any function of an administrative, judicial, or military order. He will be neither a prefect, a policeman, an officer, a judge, nor an executioner.

Why?

The individualist cannot figure among social tyrants.

What functions can he accept?

Those functions that don't harm others.

Aside from functions paid for by the government, are there harmful careers that the individualist will abstain from?

There are.

Cite a few.

Theft, banking, the exploitation of the courtesan, the exploitation of the worker.

What will the relations of the individualist be with his social inferiors?

He will respect their personality and their liberty. He will never forget that professional obligation is a fiction and that human obligation is the only moral reality. He will never forget that hierarchies are follies, and he will act naturally, not socially with the men that social falsehood affirm to be his inferiors but which nature has made his equals.

Will the individualist have many dealings with his social inferiors?

He will avoid abstentions that might upset them. But he will see little of them for fear of finding them social and unnatural; I mean for fear of finding them servile, embarrassed, or hostile.

What will the relations of an individualist be with his colleagues and his fellows?

He will be polite and accommodating with them. But he will avoid their conversation as much as he can without wounding them.

Why?

In order to defend himself against two subtle poisons: esprit de corps and professional dulling.

How will the individualist conduct himself with his social superiors?

The individualist will not forget that the words of his social superiors almost always deal with indifferent things. He will listen with indifference and respond as little as possible. He will make no objections. He won't indicate the methods that appear to him to be the best. He will avoid all useless discussion.

Why?

Because the social superior is generally a vain and irritable child.

If a social superior orders, not an indifferent thing, but an injustice or a cruelty, what will the individualist do?

He will refuse to obey.

Won't disobedience cause him to risk danger?

No. Becoming the instrument of injustice and evil is the death of reason and liberty. But disobedience to an unjust order only places the body and material resources, which are counted among indifferent things, in danger.

What will the ideas of the individualist be in the face of the forces of order?

> The individualist will mentally say to the unjust chief: you are one of the modern incarnations of the tyrant. But the tyrant can do nothing against the wise man.

Will the individualist explain his refusal to obey?

> Yes, if he thinks the social chief capable of understanding and rejecting his error. The chief is almost always incapable of understanding.

What will the individualist then do?

> The refusal to obey is the sole universal obligation in the face of an unjust order. The form of the refusal depends on my personality.

How does the individualist consider the crowd?

> The individualist considers the crowd as one of the most brutal of natural forces.

How does he act in a crowd that is causing no harm?

> He strives to not feel himself in conformity with the crowd and to not allow, even for a single instant, his personality to be drowned in it.

Why?

> In order to remain a free man. Because perhaps soon an unforeseen shock will cause the cruelty of the crowd to burst forth, and he who will have begun to feel like it, he who will truly be part of the crowd, will have difficulty separating from it at the moment of moral élan.

What will the wise man do if the crowd that he finds himself in attempts an injustice or a cruelty?

> The wise man will oppose, by all means noble and indifferent, the injustice or the cruelty.

What are the methods the wise man will not employ, even in these circumstances?

> The wise man will not descend to falsehood, prayer, or flattery.

Flattering the crowd is a powerful oratorical method. Does the wise man absolutely forbid this to himself?

> The wise man can address to the crowd, as to children, that praise that is the ironically amiable envelope of his counsels. But he will know that the limit is uncertain and adventure dangerous. He will not risk it unless he is absolutely certain not only of the firmness of his soul but also of the precise flexibility of his speech.

Will the wise man testify before tribunals?

> The wise man will never testify before tribunals.

Why?

> Testifying before tribunals for material or indifferent interests means sacrificing to the social idol and recognizing tyranny. What is more, there is cowardice in appealing to the power of all for assistance.

What will the wise man do if he is accused?

> In keeping with his character, he can tell the truth or oppose disdain and silence to social tyranny.

If the individualist recognizes his guilt, what will he say?

> He will speak of his real and natural error, and will clearly distinguish it from the apparent and social error for which he is pursued. He will add that his conscience inflicts true punishment on him for his true error. But for an apparent error, society, which only acts on indifferent things, will inflict an apparent punishment.

If the accused wise man is innocent before his conscience and guilty before the law, what will he say?

> He will explain in what way his legal crime is a natural innocence. He will speak of his contempt for the law, that organized injustice and powerlessness can do nothing to us, but only to our bodies and our wealth, which are indifferent things.

If the accused wise man is innocent before his conscience and the law, what will he say?

> He can only speak of his real innocence. If he deigns to explain these two innocences, he will declare that only the first one matters to him.

Will the wise man testify before civil tribunals?

> The wise man will not refuse his testimony to the weak oppressed.

Will the wise man testify at criminal court or before the assize court?

> Yes, if he knows a truth useful to the accused.

If the wise man knows a truth harmful to the accused, what will he do?

He will remain silent.

Why?

Because a condemnation is always an injustice, and the wise man doesn't make himself an accomplice in an injustice.

Why do you say that a condemnation is always an injustice?

Because no man has the right to inflict death on another man or to lock him in prison.

Doesn't society have rights different from those of the individual?

Society, a gathering of individuals, cannot have a right that isn't found in any individual. Zeroes, when added up, however numerous they might be, always add up to zero.

Isn't society in a state of self-defense against certain malefactors?

The right to self-defense only lasts as long as the attack itself.

Will the wise man sit on a jury?

He will always answer "no" to the first question: Is the accused guilty?

Won't that response sometimes be a lie?

That response will never be a lie.

Why?

The question of the presiding judge should be translated thusly: "Do you want us to inflict punishment on the accused?" And I am forced to answer "no," for I don't have the right to inflict punishment on anyone.

What do you think of duels?

Every appeal to violence is an evil. But the duel is a lesser evil compared to appealing to justice.

Why?

It isn't a form of cowardice; it doesn't cry out for assistance and doesn't employ the force of all against one alone.

Chapter VI: On Sacrifices to Idols

May I sacrifice to the idols of my time and country?

With indifference I can allow idols to take indifferent things from me. But I must defend what depends on me and belongs to my god.

How can I distinguish my god from idols?

My god is proclaimed by my conscience the moment it is truly my voice and not an echo. But idols are the work of society.

By what other characteristic do we recognize idols?

My god only desires the sacrifice of indifferent things. Idols demand that I sacrifice myself.

Can you explain yourself?

Idols proclaim the most servile and low expedients to be virtues: discipline and passive obedience. They demand the sacrifice of my reason and my will.

Do idols commit other injustices?

Not content with wanting to destroy what is superior to them and what I never have the right to abandon, they want me to sacrifice what doesn't belong to me at all: the life of my neighbor.

Do you know any other characteristics of idols?

The true god is eternal and immense. I must obey my reason always and everywhere. But idols vary with the time and country.

Show how idols vary with the times.

For the glory of the king I was once asked to suppress my reason and to kill my neighbor for the glory of I don't know what god foreign and external to myself. Today I am asked to make the same abominable sacrifices for the honor of the fatherland. Tomorrow they will perhaps be demanded for the honor of the race, the color, or the part of the world.

Does the idol only vary when its name changes?

As much as possible the idol avoids changing its name. But it often varies.

Cite changes in an idol that aren't accompanied by a change in name.

In a neighboring country the idol of the fatherland was Prussia; today, under the same name, the idol is Germany.

It demanded that the Prussian kill the Bavarian. Later
it demanded that the Prussian and the Bavarian kill the
Frenchman. In 1859 the Savoyard and the Niçois were at
risk of bowing before a fatherland shaped like a boot in the
near future. The hazards of diplomacy have them adore a
hexagonal fatherland. The Pole hesitates between a dead
and a living idol; the Alsatian between two living idols who
pretend to the same name of fatherland.

What are the main current idols?

In certain countries, the king or the emperor, in others
some fraud called the will of the people. Everywhere order,
the political party, religion, the fatherland, the race, the
color. We shouldn't forget public opinion, with its thousand names, from the most emphatic, honor, to the most
trivially low, the fear of "What will the neighbors say?"

Is color a dangerous idol?

The color white especially. It has managed to unite in
one cult the French, Germans, Russians, and Italians and
to obtain from these noble priests the bloody sacrifice of a
great number of Chinese.

Do you know other crimes of the color white?

It is they who have made all of Africa a hell. It
is they who destroyed the Indians of America and
lynched Negroes.

Do the adorers of the color white offer only blood to their idol?

They also offer it praise.

Speak of this praise.

It would be too long a litany. But when the color white demands a crime, the liturgy calls this crime a necessity of civilization and progress.

Is race a dangerous idol?

Yes, especially when it is allied to religion.

Speak of a few crimes of these allies.

The wars of the Medes, the conquests of the Saracens, the Crusades, the massacres of the Armenians, anti-Semitism.

What is the most demanding and universally respected idol today?

The fatherland.

Speak of the particular demands of the fatherland.

Military service and war.

Can the individualist be a soldier in time of peace?

Yes, as long as he isn't asked to commit a crime.

What does the wise man do in time of war?

The wise man never forgets the order of the true god, of reason: Thou shalt not kill. And he prefers to obey god than to obey men.

What acts will his conscience dictate to him?

The universal conscience rarely orders predetermined acts. It almost always carries prohibitions. It forbids killing or wounding your neighbor, and, on this point, it says nothing more. Methods are indifferent and constitute personal obligations.

Can the wise man remain a soldier in time of war?

The wise man can remain a soldier in time of war as long as he is certain not to allow himself to be dragged into killing or wounding.

Can the formal and open refusal to obey murderous orders become a strict obligation?

Yes, if the wise man, by his past or for other reasons finds himself in one of those situations that attract attention. Yes, for if his attitude risks scandalizing or edifying, it can lead other men toward good or evil.

Will the wise man fire at the officer who gives a murderous order?

The wise man kills no one. He knows that tyrannicide is a crime, like any willful murder.

Chapter VII: On the Relations between Morality and Metaphysics

In how many ways do we conceive the relations between morality and metaphysics?

In three ways: (1) Morality is a consequence of metaphysics, a metaphysics in action. (2) Metaphysics are a necessity and a postulate of morality. (3) Morality and metaphysics are independent of each other.

What do you think of the doctrine that makes morality depend on metaphysics?

> This doctrine is dangerous. It forces the necessary to be supported by the superfluous, the certain by the uncertain, the practical by the dream. It transforms moral life into a somnambulism trembling in fear and hope.

What do you think of the concept that renders morality and metaphysics independent of each other?

> It is the only one that can be supported from a moral point of view. This is the one that should be held to in practice.

Theoretically, don't the first two contain a portion of truth?

> Morally false, they express a probable metaphysical opinion. They signify that all realities form a whole and that there are close ties between man and the universe.

Is individualism a metaphysics?

> Individualism appears to be able to coexist with the most varied metaphysics. It appears that Socrates and the Cynics had a certain disdain for metaphysics. The Epicureans were materialists. The Stoics were pantheists.

What do you think of metaphysical doctrines in general?

> I view them as poems, and I love them for their beauty.

What constitutes the beauty of metaphysical poems?

> A metaphysic is beautiful under two conditions: (1) It should be considered as a possible and hypothetical explanation, not as a system of certainties, and it must not

deny neighboring poems. (2) It must explain everything by a harmonious reduction to unity.

What should we do in the presence of affirmative metaphysics?

We should generously strip them of the ugliness and heaviness of affirmation in order to consider them poems and systems of dreams.

What do you think of dualist metaphysics?

They are provisional explanations, semimetaphysics. There is no true metaphysic, but the only true metaphysics are those that arrive at a monism.

Is individualism an absolute morality?

Individualism is not a morality. It is only the strongest moral method we know, the most impregnable citadel of virtue and happiness.

Is individualism fitting for all men?

There are men who are invincibly repelled by the seeming harshness of individualism. These should choose another moral method.

How can I know if individualism is not appropriate to my nature?

If after a loyal attempt at individualism I feel myself to be unhappy, if I don't feel that I am in the true refuge, and if I am troubled with pity for myself and others, I should flee individualism.

Why?

Because this method, too strong for my weakness, will lead me to egoism or discouragement.

By what method can I create a moral life for myself if I am too weak for the individualist method?

By altruism, by love, by pity.

Will this method lead me to acts different from those of an individualist?

Truly moral beings all carry out the same acts and, even more, all abstain from the same acts. Every moral being respects the life of other men; no moral being occupies himself with earning useless wealth, and so forth.

What will the altruist say who uselessly attempted to employ the individualist method?

He'll say to himself: "I have the same path to follow. I have done nothing but leave behind an armor too heavy for me and that attracted violent blows from destiny and men. And I took up the pilgrim's staff. But I will always remember that I hold this staff to support myself, and not to strike others."

[From *Petite manuel individualiste*. Paris: Librairie française, 1905.]

GEORGES PALANTE

Nietzsche believed that reading a philosopher's works was equivalent to reading his autobiography. Seldom is this as startlingly true as in the works of Georges Palante. As Michel Onfray said in his preface to the 2004 edition of Palante's collected philosophical works, "Autobiography reveals itself in each word, behind each thesis. The writing, the ideas, the composition of all his books, his references, his citations, everything is mobilized in an attempt to sublimate, in the Freudian sense of the term, an existence dramatically placed under the sign of melancholy, of psychic and physical slowness, of ugliness, of fatigue, of pain and suffering."

Palante, born in 1862 in a town in the Pas-de-Calais that would be totally destroyed during World War I, spent virtually his entire life in the provinces, and this physical distance from Paris, the center of French thought, was echoed in his own sui generis philosophy.

Thrown back on himself by acromegaly, which deformed him physically, giving him abnormally long arms, Palante produced a philosophy that places the individual at the center of all. A victim of ostracism in life, his philosophy has no place for collective action; in Palante's philosophy, life is despair. It is a world of great men who will ultimately be laid low, of the ineluctable crushing of any individual who tries to climb out of the enveloping muck. His life was a trail of personal disasters: his dreadful marriage to a woman who misunderstood him and destroyed his unfinished works after his death; his awful disease, whose resultant deformity subjected him to ridicule by those around him; his misguided attempt at academic distinction, which ended in bitter failure; and his oversensitivity, which led to a duel with a former friend and ultimately to his suicide in 1925. A former pupil of Palante's, Louis Guilloux, wrote a moving volume of memoirs of the philosopher and included a Palante-inspired character in his autobiographical novel Le Sang Noir.

All of his misfortunes fed Palante's genius. His philosophy, founded on his failed personal dreams and miseries, is so fecund that it touches us even today.

Individualism

As is the case elsewhere, the tendency to underestimate the individual has made itself felt in the intellectual field. Solitary thought—invention—has been deprecated to the profit of collective thought—imitation—preached under the eternal word of solidarity. The horror of the previously untried, of intellectual and aesthetic originality, is a characteristic trait of Latin races. We love regimented thought, conformist and decent meditations. A

German writer, Laura Marholm, accurately analyzed this contemporary tendency:

> Intellectual cowardice is a universal trait. No one dares makes a decisive statement concerning his milieu. No one any longer allows himself an original thought. Original thought only dares present itself when it is supported by a group: it has to have gathered together several adherents in order to dare show itself. You must be one of many before daring to speak. This is an indication of universal democratization, a democratization that is still at its beginnings, and is characterized by a reaction against international capital, which until now has had at its disposal all the means of military and legislative defense. No one dares to rely on himself alone. An idea that contravenes received ideas almost never manages to make itself known. The propagation of an antipathetic idea is circumscribed and hindered by a thousand anonymous censors, among which the official censorship of the state has only a minor role.

The result of this tendency is that we no longer exist and think for ourselves. We think according to hearsay and slogans.

It is especially from the moral point of view that the crushing of personal egoism by group egoism is intolerable. We too well know the pettiness of the group spirit, the gregarious coalitions engaged above all in fighting against superior individualities, their solidarity in irresponsibility, all these forms of diminished humanity.

It is the same with perfect solidarity as it is with absolute justice, absolute altruism, absolute monism. These are abstract principles untranslatable in real terms. Each man has his particular understanding of solidarity, of justice, his own way to interpret the *fas* and the *nefas* in keeping with his coterie, class, and other interests.

"As soon as an idea is set loose," said Remy de Gourmont,

If we thus set it nakedly in circulation, in its voyage around the world it joins all kinds of parasitic vegetation. Sometimes the original organism disappears, entirely devoured by the egoistic colonies that develop there. An amusing example of these deviations in thought was given by the corporation of house painters at the ceremony called "The Triumph of the Republic." The workers carried around a banner where their demands for justice were summed up in this cry: "Down with ripolin!" You must know that ripolin is a prepared paint that anyone can spread across woodwork. We can thus understand the sincerity of this wish and its ingenuity. Ripolin here represents injustice and oppression; it's the enemy, the devil. We all have our own ripolin and we color according to our needs the abstract ideas that, without this, would be of no personal use to us.

The ideal is soiled in contact with reality:
Pearl before falling, and mire after.
[From *l'anarchie*, no. 323, June 15, 1911.]

The Relationship between Pessimism and Individualism

The century that just ended is undoubtedly the one in which pessimism found its most numerous, its most varied, its most vigorous, and its most systematic interpreters. In addition, during that century individualism was expressed with exceptional intensity by representatives of high quality.

It would be interesting to bring together these two forms of thought, dominant in our era; to ask what is the logical or sentimental connection that exists between them, and to what degree pessimism engenders individualism and individualism engenders pessimism.

But the question thus posed is too general. There are many kinds of pessimism and many kinds of individualism. Among the latter there is one that in no way implies pessimism, and that is the doctrinaire individualism that issues from the French Revolution and to which so many moralists, jurists, and politicians of our century are attached. This individualism could take as its motto the phrase of Wilhelm von Humboldt that John Stuart Mill chose as the epigraph of his essay *On Liberty*: "The grand, leading principle, towards which every argument unfolded in these pages directly converges, is the absolute and essential importance of human development in its richest diversity." Individualists of this kind believe that all human individuals can harmonically develop in society, that their very diversity is a guarantee of the richness and beauty of human civilization.

These individualists are rationalists. They have faith in reason, in the principles of order, of unity, and of harmony. They are idealists: they have faith in an ideal of social justice. Unitarian and egalitarian, they believe, despite individual differences and inequalities, in the profound and real unity of humankind. These individualists are "humanists" in the sense that Stirner gives to this word: solidarists, socialists, if we take this latter term in its largest sense. Their individualism is turned outward, toward society. It's a social individualism, in the sense that it doesn't separate the individual from society, which they don't place in opposition to each other. On the contrary, they always consider the individual as a social element that harmonizes with the all and that only exists in function of the all. We will not insist on this individualism, which obviously implies a more or less firm social optimism.

The individualism we have in mind here is completely different. This individualism is not a political, juridical, and moral doctrine, but a psychological and moral attitude, a form of sensibility, a personal sensation of life and a personal will to life.

It is impossible to fix in a definition all the traits, all the degrees, all the nuances of this psychological disposition. It affects a special tone in every soul in which it makes itself known.

We can say that as a personal sensation of life, individualism is the sentiment of uniqueness, of individuality in what it possesses of the differentiating, the private, and the unreveal-able. Individualism is an appeal to the interiority of sentiment, to individual inspiration in the face of social conventions and ready-made ideas. Individualism implies a sentiment of personal infallibility, an idea of intellectual and sentimental superiority, of inner artistocratism; of irreducible difference between a self and another: the idea of uniqueness. Individualism is a return to the self and a gravitation toward the self.

As personal will to life, individualism is a desire to "be one-self," according to the desire of a character from Ibsen (*Peer Gynt*), a desire for independence and originality. The individualist wants to be his own maker, his own provider of truth and illusion; his own builder of truth and illusion; his own builder of dreams; his own builder and demolisher of ideals. This wish for originality can, incidentally, be more or less energetic, more or less demand-ing, more or less ambitious. More or less happy, too, according to the quality and the value of the individuality in cause, according to the amplitude of the thought and according to the intensity of, the will to, individual might.

Be it as personal sensation of life or as personal will to life, individualism is or tends to be antisocial: if it is not so from the start, it later and inevitably becomes so. A sentiment of the pro-found uniqueness of the self, a desire for originality and independence, individualism cannot help but provoke the sentiment of a silent struggle between the individual self and society. In fact, the tendency of every society is to reduce the sentiment of in-dividuality as much as possible: to reduce uniqueness through conformity; spontaneity through discipline; instantaneousness of the self through caution; sincerity of sentiment through the lack of sincerity inherent in any socially defined function; confidence and pride in the self through the humiliation inseparable from any kind of social training. This is why individualism necessar-ily contains the sentiment of a conflict between its self and the general self. Individualism becomes here a principle of passive or active inner resistance, of silent or declared opposition to society, a refusal to submit oneself to it, a distrust of it. In its essence, individualism holds in contempt and negates the social bond.

We can define it as a will to isolation, a sentimental and intellectual, theoretical, and practical commitment to withdraw from society, if not in fact—following the examples of the solitaries of the Thebeiad and the more modern one of Thoreau—at least in sprit and intention, by a kind of interior and voluntary retreat. This distancing from society, this voluntary moral isolation that we can practice in the very heart of society, can assume the form of indifference and resignation as well as that of revolt. It can also assume the attitude of the spectator, the contemplative attitude of the thinker in an ivory tower. But there is always in this acquired indifference, in this resignation or this spectatorial isolation, a remnant of interior revolt.

A feeling of uniqueness and a more or less energetic expression of the will to personal power, a will to originality, a will to independence, a will to insubordination and revolt, a will to isolation and to withdrawal into the self. Sometimes also a will to supremacy, to the deployment of force on and against others, but always with a return to the self, with a sentiment of personal infallibility, with an indestructible confidence in oneself, even in defeat, even in the failure of hopes and ideals. Intransigence, inaccessibility of internal conviction, fidelity to oneself up to the bitter end. Fidelity to one's misunderstood ideas, to one's impregnable and unassailable will: individualism is all this, either globally or in detail, this element or that, this nuance or that predominating according to the circumstances and the case.

Individualism, understood as we just expressed it, that is, as an internal disposition of the soul, individualism as a sensation and will, is no longer, like the individualism of which we spoke above, like political and juridical individualism, turned outward and subordinated to social life, to its constraints, its demands and obligations. It is turned inward. It places itself at the beginning or seeks refuge in the end in the unbreakable and intangible interior being.

To say that there is a close psychological relationship between the individualist and pessimist sensibilities is almost stating the obvious. Pessimism supposes a basic individualism. It supposes the interiority of sentiment, the return to the self (almost always painful) that is the essence of individualism. While optimism is nothing but an abstract metaphysical thesis, the echo of doctrinal hearsay, pessimism is a sensation of lived life; it comes from the inner, from an individual psychology. It proceeds from what is most intimate in us: the ability to suffer. It predominates among those of a solitary nature who live withdrawn into themselves and see social life as pain. Born pessimists, the great artists and theoreticians of suffering lived alone and as strangers in the midst of men, retrenched in their self as if in a fortress from which they let fall an ironic and haughty gaze on the society of their fellows. And so, it is not by accident but by virtue of an intimate psychological correlation that pessimism is accompanied by a tendency toward egotistic isolation.

Conversely, the individualist spirit is almost necessarily accompanied by pessimism. Does not experience as old as the world teach us that in nature the individual is sacrificed to the species? That in society it is sacrificed to the group? Individualism arrives at a resigned or hopeless noting of the antinomies that arise between the individual and the species, on one hand, and between the individual and society, on the other.

Life doubtless perpetually triumphs over this antinomy, and the fact that, despite it all, humanity continues to live might appear to be an unarguable reply refuting both pessimism and individualism. But this is not certain. For if humanity as a species and as a society pursues its destiny without worrying about individuals' complaints or revolts, individualism does not die for all that. Always defeated, never tamed, it is incarnated in souls of a special caliber, imbued with the sentiment of their uniqueness and strong in their will to independence. Individualism suffers a defeat in every individual who dies after having served ends and surrendered to forces that are beyond him. But he survives himself through the generations, gaining in force and clarity as the human will to life intensifies, diversifies, and becomes refined in individual consciousness. It is thus that the dual consistency of pessimism and individualism, indissolubly united and intertwined, is affirmed.

Nevertheless, it is possible that this psychological connection that we believe we have discovered between pessimism and individualism is nothing but an a priori view. If instead of reasoning about psychological likelihoods we consult the history of ideas of the nineteenth century we will perhaps see that the relationship of ideas that we have just indicated is neither as simple nor as consistent as at first appears. We must penetrate in detail the different forms of pessimism and individualism and more closely analyze their relationship if we want to arrive at precise ideas.

[From *Pessimisme et Invidualisme*. Paris: Alcan, 1914.]

The Future of Pessimism and Individualism

Everything in current social evolution indicates an increased reinforcement of society's powers, an increasingly marked tendency toward the encroachment of the collective on the individual.

Everything equally indicates that on the part of most individuals this encroachment will be less and less felt and will provoke less and less resistance and rebellion. Social conformism and optimism will thus clearly have the last word. Society will emerge victorious over the individual. There will come a moment when social chains will wound almost no one, lacking people sufficiently in love with independence and sufficiently individualized to feel these chains and suffer from them. Lacking combatants, the combat will come to an end. The small independent minority will become increasingly small.

But however small it might be, it will suffer from increased social pressure. It will represent, in this time of almost perfect conformism and generalized social contentment, pessimism and individualism.

[From *Pessimisme et Individualisme*. Paris: Alcan, 1914.]

VICTOR SERGE

Few people have lived as eventful and tumultuous a life as that of Victor Serge. The road he followed was one few took in the twentieth century, and precisely because of his varied political commitments he has had the most lasting impact among those included here.

Born Victor Kibalchich in Brussels in 1890, he was the son of impoverished Russian exiles, related (though it is still unclear to what degree) to Nicolas Kibalchich, one of the participants in the Narodnik assassination of Tsar Alexander II. The spirit of the Russian Narodniki was to guide him throughout his life, and in his Memoirs of a Revolutionary *he said they allowed him to avoid many of the ideological pitfalls of his individualist comrades.*

He began his political life at fifteen in the youth organization of the Belgian Workers' Party, along with a group of friends, including Raymond Callemin,

Jean De Boë, and Édouard Carouy who would later join him in anarchism and become bandits in the Bonnot Gang. While living on an anarchist commune, he learned the printing trade that would help him survive his turbulent life and began writing for the newspaper Le Communiste, *which later became* Le Révolté. *By the time he was eighteen, he was writing articles impregnated with individualist ideas, including the defense of anarchists in London and Belgium who had fought off and killed police.*

He moved to Paris in mid-1909 and began writing for l'anarchie *under a variety of pseudonyms (Le Rétif, Ralph, Yor) and giving talks at various anarchist study circles. By 1911 he was editor of* l'anarchie, *around which were congregated his Brussels friends (he claimed he had demanded they leave the paper because of their juvenile and dangerous ideas). With the outbreak of the Bonnot Gang's crime wave, he was, in the pages of the paper at least, an outspoken apologist for even their most brutal shootings.*

The police had strong reason to believe that the criminals involved in the Bonnot Affair were involved in l'anarchie, *and during a search of the paper's offices police found guns that had been stolen during one of the gang's robberies. As a result, Victor and his companion Rirette Maîtrejean, who coedited the paper, were arrested on January 31, 1912. He was held for five years, being convicted at the Bonnot trial for possession of stolen goods. He had been added to the defendants, the rest of whom were the surviving gunmen, as the theoretician of illegalism, but at the trial he denied ever having supported the idea (despite having written numerous articles doing*

*just that) and separated himself completely from his
codefendants.*

*While in jail, the process of distancing himself
from his anarchist individualist milieu continued,
and when he was released in 1917 and expelled from
France he went to Barcelona, where he participated
in a workers' uprising. After being imprisoned again
in France for returning against an expulsion order,
he completed his move away from individualism and
moved to the USSR, where he immediately became
an important propagandist for the Bolsheviks. In articles aimed at French anarchists, he attempted to justify Bolshevik actions and more importantly expressed
the hope that anarchists could save Bolshevism from
its dictatorial and socially reactionary tendencies.*

*After Lenin's death, Serge supported Trotsky and
as a result was expelled from the party in 1928. In
1933 he was arrested and sent to Oranienburg. As a
result of a massive campaign, he was released from
detention and expelled from the USSR. Active in the
Trotskyist Opposition, he soon fell out with Trotsky
and spent the rest of his life, which included further
exile to Mexico, as a freelance radical, supporting the
POUM in Spain, condemning the Stalinist show tri-
als, and performing what he called his "double duty,"
protecting the revolution from its enemies without
and its enemies within. He died suddenly of heart
failure in 1947.*

The Communards

March is here, and with it the return of the anniversary of mad hopes, of the furious impulses and butcheries of the Commune, our last effort toward revolution. Forty-one years after the frightening experience, the same illusions give rise in the same people to the same dangerous hope. For if, as the proverb says, we live on hope, it also happens that we die of it; that for his dreams man puts his life at risk—and loses.

One of the hopes most deeply rooted in the popular soil is that in the magic virtues of insurrection. This is only natural. It is derived from the feeling of confidence inspired by force. What is force not capable of? The people, who suffer its rigors, upon whom the privileged and adventurous minorities daily exercise their power, learn in this way the immeasurable value of the solid fist, the saber, and guile. These are the means by which they are tamed, and they count on these things alone to have their day and time. There's nothing surprising in the fact that such a faith should preserve its prestige despite the worst lessons. The belief in revolution is nothing but confidence in the power of brute force, a confidence vulgarized and depicted for the use of the crowd. A defeat presages nothing; it doesn't extinguish the hope for victory in the defeated. The Commune died in 1871 under Gallifet's boot?[1] Well, Long Live the Insurrection!

It isn't the intelligence of the popular crowd that expresses itself in this way, but its instinct, and this is why reasoning has no more success with these believers than the costly experiences of yesterday and the day before.

Have there been more conclusive experiences? Revolutions have never achieved their goals. They have sometimes "succeeded," but in reality, they have neither destroyed what they wanted to destroy nor constructed anything new or better. In fact, they've only succeeded when bourgeois liberals and intriguers have joined the insurgent people. Insurrections invariably fail without

---

1   The Marquis de Gallifet was a general responsible for much of the brutal repression of the Paris Commune. —ed.

the assistance of these forces. It was because they were abandoned at the last minute by the wealthy "moderates" that the rebels of Moscow in 1905 were cut to pieces despite their heroism, and it's because the republican petite bourgeoisie didn't agree to back it that the Barcelona uprising was put down in three days. The revolutionary minority, the working people and the masses, lack not only the organizational qualities and the knowledge necessary for the success of a political—and even more, a social—upheaval, but even more, they are lacking in the resources, men, and money. There is no doubt that a revolution can triumph with the cooperation of shop owners, liberal and sympathetic philanthropists, lawyers, and a few perspicacious bankers. But these messieurs will only intervene if they have good reason to do so; in general, they snatch the movement. And when friends are installed in city hall, the barracks, the town halls promising decisive reforms as is right, the game has been won. But by whom?

Is this not the abridged history of the recent Portuguese revolution? The proletarians of Lisbon and Porto, socialist and anarchist, who paid for the republic with their persons, only understood their role four months later when the soldiers of the new government—their sons—fired on them. Exactly like the old one. But why insist? Is this not the synthesis of the history of the most famous revolution, of the Great French Revolution, of which all that is left are some refrains: "*Ah, ça ira, ça ira . . .*"[2] swiped by a brilliant bandit, by men who were soldiers by chance, and by speechmakers. . . .

* * *

And yet the Commune was the "great federation of pain," as Jules Vallès said. And if it didn't have a general staff specialized in organization and social war to guide it toward a propitious destiny, it had strategists, several of whom had gone to the excellent school of Blanqui—the true Imprisoned One—and it came at the

---

2   From the chorus of one of the songs of the French Revolution. "Everything will be fine . . ." as the "aristocrats are hung from the lampposts." —ed.

right moment, rich in horrors, backed by the anger of a population desolated by war having a disorganized government to fight.
It was heroic, stubborn, the federation of pains, and heroically
incompetent.

It was typical: humanitarian despite the war and as if war can
be made by half; honest, as our revolutionaries brag of being, for
whom there is no worse insult than being confused with "crooks";
honest and respectful of the money of others, a thousand times
more than the other side was of the lives of the Communards; futile, divided by the rivalries of improvised generals and legislators;
divided also by mistrust, though they hadn't yet invented the revolutionary security service; heroic, to be sure, and admirably so.
... But can the people do better? Lacking in education, not used
to thinking, not knowing how to count on themselves, needing
for the least effort to be in groups, led, federated—alas—could
the workers and beggars of 1912 do better? They would still have
the resource of bravely, unblinkingly having themselves killed for
their beautiful dream. They'll have only that resource. ...

Because they aren't the strongest, because their real enemies
are within them. Their inconsistency, their sentimentality, their
ignorance places them at the mercy of eager soldiers, fierce politicians, and loudmouths. A society is a complex organism that
takes centuries to form and perfect itself and that only succeeds
in doing so by absorbing countless energies, competencies, and
talents. You would like to remake this work in a few days, you
race of "serfs" and "villeins" in whom the religious and authoritarian past left a durable imprint? If you caress this dream, other
Communards will pass before the wall!

And we will perhaps admire them, but we won't follow them.
More than they, because we are more conscious, we have a profound love of life and the invincible desire to take our part of the
feasts under the sun But in order to become stronger we have to
become more circumspect, and our goals are located in the here
and now and not in the beyond, in the reality of our individual
lives and not in the fiction of "humanity."

Man must live instead of giving himself, offering himself in
a holocaust to the dream! Let his courage allow him finally to

become a free man, ardent and noble, instead of succumbing as a vain hero to (perhaps) modify the name of a tyranny. And if he falls, it's better that he does so on his own account. And if he succeeds, his life as a rebel will contribute to the evolution of the social environment at least as much as will the deaths of the others.

[From: *l'anarchie*, March 28, 1912.]

A Head Will Fall

Nothing is more repugnant than the macabre judicial comedy that all too often ends in a new exploit of the guillotine, which is contrary to vulgar common sense, revolting to feelings, and, from the social point of view, as unjust as it is immoral.

In vain does vulgar common sense demonstrate that a wound isn't healed by leaving behind a stump, that one crime—and a murder coldly decided on and prepared by the official representatives of society is a crime par excellence—doesn't repair another and in no way prevents the future crimes that contemporary illogic renders inevitable. Logic and common sense! Only a few eccentrics—the anarchists—timidly attempt to conform to them.

Revolting? Yes, the death penalty is as revolting as can be. In a few tragic pages of his *Mêlée Sociale* Clemenceau related the horror of executions. He then hurried to forget them (one forgets so many things when one becomes a minister). Fifteen years after he described it, the sinister scene in the gray-and-red dawn of La Roquette Prison is being replayed. It only revolts dreamers like us.

Unjust, immoral. … Big words that are laughed at in the twentieth century of all-out civilization. Do we ever see those who rule through the force of injustice seek to be just in their acts? And do we ever see the imbeciles who live under their influence and support them aspire to anything? Come now! Justice and morality are things to be taught in stultifying classrooms so that children learn not to rebel later on.

So instead of worrying about this nonsense they judge, they sentence, and they kill. Journalists, speculating on the blood-thirsty hysteria of the mob, demand heads; magistrates, symbolically garbed in purple, deliberate, split hairs, discuss before deciding if the wretch who stands before them will through their sinister good humor be sent to Maroni's garden of tortures or put in the hands of their compere Deibler.[3] This depends strictly on these gentlemen's mood. All that's needed is for the grocer who presides over the jury to be a cuckold, for his business to go badly, for him to have a corn on his foot and a man's fate is sealed. The good people applaud. The most sensitive rejoice when the clemency of the judges has destined a poor bugger to torture instead of sending him straight to his death. But when a head falls, most of them are delirious with joy.

To judge, to condemn, to torture or guillotine are all as idiotic as they are useless, not to say harmful. But who cares? Most people understand nothing about this. It's the veritable apotheosis of imbecility: magistrates, judges, executioners, soldiers, none of them understand a thing.

Others, frightened by crimes whose tide is rising and which threaten them, feel themselves to be in danger and strike out blindly. Not understanding that repressive ferocity is pointless and that it is the cause of crime that must be attacked; that from the moment that people are hungry, lack air and sun, and break down in factories and barracks it is inevitable that they will rob and murder. But go talk of correct reasoning, of science, of determinism to people who are confused by fear and are enslaved to petty interests.

This time will be like all the others. The judicial machine has functioned, and unless the buxom Fallières[4] has, following some truculent banquet, the "humanitarian" fantasy of sending Liabeuf to the galleys, a head will fall.[5] But this time it's not the head of some unlucky soul or a brute. ...

---

3 The public executioner. —ed.

4 President of France from 1906 to 1913. —ed.

5 Jean-Jacques Liabeuf was a shoemaker guillotined on July 2, 1910, after killing two policemen in revenge for having been unjustly imprisoned as a pimp. His cause was taken up by a significant part of the Left, particularly the anarchists. —ed.

This was a very simple story. The vice squad cops, who are, as Clemenceau so picturesquely said, "official scoundrels," had sated themselves on this victim in order to justify the salary society allocates to them for the brutalizing of prostitutes and the hunting down of nonmilitary pimps. They thought it less dangerous to arrest an inoffensive passerby. When dealing with an authentic pimp one must always fear being stabbed. With this worker, they thought, impunity was certain. The little young man protested. A waste of time. If all citizens are equal according to the text of the law, in practice no word can counterbalance the words spoken by a cop. "Pimp!" the cops said, just as on other occasions they said "Demonstrator!" That was enough.

Luckily, it happens that the police sometimes choose poorly. They arrest someone who it happens is not completely spineless and is less fearful than a certified revolutionary. A good bugger who has guarded intact the notion of his individual dignity and whose energy isn't satisfied with jeremiads and has enough determination to move from words to acts, even if this involves a serious risk.

This is a summary of the Liabeuf Affair.

Personally, there's nothing about Liabeuf to interest us. Honest worker or *apache*, it's no difference to us: the distinction is too subtle for anarchist logic to take pleasure in.[6] Certified honest people are often the worst rats, and among those called apaches there can unquestionably be found people of greater individual value. Nevertheless, taken as a whole, one can say that the ones are no better than the others, which flatters neither of them. As concerns Liabeuf, it doesn't mean a thing to us to know what he really was. But we must recognize the energy he demonstrated in a situation where we are used to seeing cowardice.

Viewed on its own, his act was an anarchist act.

He wanted to kill the policemen Maugras and Mors, who had sent him to prison and prohibited his residing in Paris. Outside any purely sentimental considerations—which have their

---

6   "Apache" is French slang for a hoodlum. —ed.

importance—this sentence off-handedly delivered was of a kind to upset an entire existence.

The "official scoundrels" of morality—ministerial style—caused him to suffer an irreparable humiliation and brutally intervened in his life, whose course they changed. I understand that a man of a vigorous character thought vengeance was absolutely necessary. But was this really vengeance? Wasn't it rather an act of legitimate defense?

They beat him. He defended himself. What isn't normal is that such cases occur so rarely. What is abnormal is the cowardly indifference of the countless unfortunates who suffer without balking the humiliations of the many valets of capital and authority. Clearly the secular school and the barracks have obtained magnificent results: they have created in the overwhelming majority of those whose youth they've ground down the mentality of slaves they can use at will.

Healthy men will never forget that for the individual defending his life is a primordial duty.

As biology teaches us, in a well-constituted organism every attack that puts its organism in danger is immediately followed by a vigorous reaction. Sociologists teach us that in the free communities of primitives, where slavery was not yet established, to each denial of justice committed to the detriment of someone, to every affront, to every threat, the insulted individual responded with an equivalent reaction. For it is an inexorable law of nature that any being incapable of defending itself will disappear.

And this law is rigorously verified in social life. The man who doesn't defend himself, accepting the oppression society places on him without reacting, always disappears. There are those who simply die, murdered by tuberculosis or in service to the fatherland in Madagascar, in Tonkin, or wherever. There are those who peacefully end their days in bed at age sixty, without having lived a single moment of their own. From their first step till their final shudder they never had their own will, they were never individualities. He was Mr. John Doe, Mr. Everyman whose existence no one bothered with and whose death will pass unnoticed. He never struck back; he passively accepted the blows that quickly turned him into a gray, unassuming, flabby silhouette: someone shapeless.

The person who wants to live, to seize in the here and now his share of the sun, of flowers and joy, must affirm himself, must know how to walk alone, think with his own mind. He must act freely, react without truce against the fetters placed by an absurd social organization on the satisfaction of his most elementary needs and most logical wishes. Resisting enslavement is a condition sine qua non of the fulfillment of individual life.

In a word: defending oneself. Returning blow for blow. There are obstacles, there are circumstances where force is the only weapon that can be used.

Liabeuf, though wanting to strike the direct artisans of his misfortune, struck by chance the agents who arrested him.

There is no worse wrong that can be committed against an individual than that of depriving him of his freedom. Even death is less serious, for it is not painful, while imprisonment constitutes a continuous, abominable torture. We can call it a "death that is granted consciousness," and even this metaphor is powerless to explain how horrible for a human being the abolition of all that characterizes life for him is.

Rebellion is essential against this ultimate assault. The sole fact of depriving a man of his freedom for an hour justifies the strongest reprisals on his part. What am I saying? The mere act of a policeman putting his hand on your shoulder, because it signifies an attack on the human personality, is on its own sufficient reason to justify any form of revolt.

I will end by citing the words that legend attributed to Duval, one of the first anarchist militants in France.[7] He is supposed to have responded to the cop's sacramental "In the name of the law, I arrest you," by this phrase that followed the shot from his revolver: "In the name of freedom, I eliminate you!"

[From *l'anarchie*, May 12, 1910.]

---

7   Clément Duval (1850–1935), illegalist anarchist, member of the band called the Panther of Batignolles. —ed.

RIRETTE MAÎTREJEAN

Rirette Maîtrejean (1887–1968) was not a great the-
oretician of anarchism, nor did she play a leading role
in the movement. And yet, her life was an exemplary
one, most of it that of a rank-and-file militant who
lived the dramas of anarchist individualism, was per-
manently scarred by them, and yet never recanted her
belief in a libertarian future. This series of articles
published in 1913 in the Parisian daily Le Temps,
later published several times in book form, provides
a unique and invaluable portrait of life at the heart
of the movement, at its main journal, l'anarchie,
which she briefly edited along with her lover Victor
Kibalchich, later Victor Serge. It was at that news-
paper's offices that she came to know the anarchist
bandits known as the Bonnot Gang. Her depiction
of the members, of their personal and dietary foibles,
sometimes seems exaggerated, and one can question
the total accuracy of some of the tales she recounts
here. But virtually every story she tells, every eccen-
tricity she mocks, can be found somewhere in the texts
of the movement. There are other books by others who
knew the Bonnot Gang and their circle; none of them

equal Rirette's, and none, with the exception of Victor Serge's tendentious and self-serving account in his memoirs, were written by someone who knew them so well or who was put on trial along with them.

Rirette Maîtrejean was born in 1887 and moved to Paris from her native Corrèze around 1904. Almost immediately she became involved in individualist anarchist circles, and after being the companion of the writer and militant Mauricius she married the saddler Louis Maîtrejean, with whom she had the two daughters mentioned in the following piece. Maîtrejean was an illegalist and was arrested for counterfeiting, after which she connected with Victor Kibalchich.

Briefly the editor in 1909 of l'anarchie, *in 1911 she took over the editorship full-time from André Lorulot. As recounted below, Maîtrejean and Kibalchich were arrested for their involvement with the Bonnot Gang, specifically for the possession of a stolen pistol. Maîtrejean was found innocent of all charges, and Victor, found guilty, spent five years in prison.*

During that time, Serge wrote Rirette 528 letters, and in order to allow Rirette to visit, they married. As Serge's unpublished correspondence reveals, Rirette was not as assiduous in writing and visiting as he would have liked, and though they moved together to Spain upon his release from prison in 1917, she was unable to find work and they went their separate ways.

Rirette ceased militant activity and followed the advice Victor gave her to abandon the world of individualist anarchism, though she remained faithful to the greater cause. She worked as a proofreader (a heavily anarchist trade), was close to the anarcho-syndicalists, and exerted a tremendous influence on a young Algerian writer she befriended, Albert Camus. So close were they that when Camus fled Paris in the exodus that followed the German invasion of France in 1940, he did so with Rirette. They remained friends until the writer's death in 1960, and her influence on his political ideas is stressed in the volume edited by *Lou Marin*, Albert Camus: Écrits libertaires.

Rirette died in 1968 at a nursing home outside Paris.

Her "Memories of Anarchy" were published as a serial in the Parisian daily Le Matin *between August 19 and August 31, 1913, when the ideological and personal wounds of the Bonnot Gang were still fresh.*

Serge wrote a novel after his move to Russia about his anarchist days. However, the manuscript was lost, confiscated by the Soviet authorities. Lacking that, "Memories of Anarchy" is perhaps the best direct testimony we have about the daily life of the circle that included the Bonnot Gang.

Memories of Anarchy

*In Which Rirette Maître jean Experiences
Her First Disappointments*

It's not as if you've had any experience when you're twenty years old. One can only have that of others, and as everyone knows, the only experiences that count are those obtained at your own expense. Even so, I was able to make a few observations. I noted the profound aversion my comrades expressed for all forms of wage labor, but with this attitude paydays were rare. And if counterfeit coin is one remedy, solid cash also has its value, though we rarely saw any of it. As for eating, we thought of it more than we did it. We ate little and drank only water. It's extraordinary, the quantity of water certain anarchists consumed for internal compared to external usage. Being a water drinker and a vegetarian are two characteristics of the perfect anarchist. They couldn't bear to see killed meat on their plate: in their hearts is engraved the motto "Be kind to animals."

Callemin,[1] Garnier,[2] and Bonnot[3] would under no conditions have eaten steak or drunk a glass of wine. I'm speaking of the time when they were only anarchists.

I've not yet managed to understand how, with so few needs, they ended up with such great appetites.

Mandatory Hospitality

For eighteen months of the three years I lived with Maître jean[4] we had the daily visit of a friend of my husband named Chilon: he

---

1   Raymond Callemin (1890–1913), Belgian-born Bonnot Gang member. Known as Raymond-la-Science for his obsession with the scientific nature of life and anarchism. —ed.

2   Octave Garnier (1889–1913), anarchist burglar, counterfeiter, and draft evader. Member of the Bonnot Gang. —ed.

3   Jules Bonnot (1876–1912), leader of the illegalist anarchist gang that bore his name. Killed in a bitter battle with the police in Choisy-le-Roi. —ed.

4   Louis Maître jean (1880–?), anarchist and counterfeiter. He remained an

wasn't Greek, only anarchist. Without needing to be invited he sat at our table, took the choicest morsels, and drank three-quarters of the wine. He customarily said: "Among anarchists there's no reason to be embarrassed." And when he was feeling particularly honest he would say with no shame: "I like just as much to live off anarchist suckers as bourgeois suckers."

As work grew scarce so did money. "I'd like to think," I said to my husband, "that you're going to tell that freeloader to be on his way."

Maîtrejean promised he would but never did. At 7:00 on the dot, as was his habit, our guest made his entry. I'd only set two places. Without demanding any explanation Chilon sat down and ate his soup. "That was really good," he said as he left. We had no choice but to move without leaving a forwarding address.

Everything for the Idea

Not to work: this, for the anarchist, was everything.

He'll spend five or six hours spying out a tin of sardines and will think his days is complete when it will have passed from the grocer's inventory to his pocket. This might be fine in theory; in practice, the charms of such an existence can be argued against. It's true that people like what they like, and it must never be forgotten that we lived above all for the idea.

Three things that do not always go well together: How many comrades I've met who spoke without thinking. As for thinking, not everyone can do it. Simplistic and unpolished workers made a stab at it. They thought that in doing so they were living their lives. I felt great pity for them.

I was ripe to go over to the camp of the intellectuals. I had barely come of age.

Anarchist Incompatibility of Humor

And so, I left Maîtrejean. At first, I felt a vague regret: after all, he was a good man, a good worker. For the past three years, every

---

active militant into the 1950s. —ed.

Saturday he had brought home a nice paycheck. My two daughters and I lacked nothing.

What did I hold against him?

Nothing specific. At the very most an anarchist incompatibility of humor. Our minds didn't meet. Any elevated idea gave him vertigo, while I was only happy at the heights. It was the sole and only complaint I had against this man who, for three years, had put up with my demands. Abandoned, Maîtrejean stopped working. Did he still think of me? Did he want to reconquer me? Did he want to peremptorily show that he, too, was a perfect illegalist? Perhaps.

One day I learned that he had been arrested as a counterfeiter. In his previous profession as a saddler he earned 10 francs a day. In his new profession he never made more than 30 francs a week. No one is more exploited than a counterfeiter. Four years of prison crowned his efforts.

I never think of the father of my children without a feeling of profound sorrow and sympathy mixed with pity.

There I was setting out to live my life. I headed straight for the intellectuals: at least with them you can talk. Conversation occupies an important place in anarchist life.

I had to choose a label. Would I be an individualist or a communist? There was hardly a choice. Among the communists woman is reduced to a role where no one ever talks to her, even before. It's true that among the individualists things are hardly any different. Even so, I preferred individualism. I can't say as much about illegalism. Its risks seem to me to be out of proportion to its advantages.

A speaker—in that world, which recognizes no authority, that's what leaders are called—saw to rounding out my anarchist education. Never was a student more fervent or more docile. What do you expect? I burned with a sacred flame.

I assiduously followed the Causeries Populaires in the Cité d'Angoulême [in Paris' 11th arrondissement].

It was a picturesque spot: at the end of a dark courtyard where poverty oozed from the flaking paving stones there was an opening in a tottering wall onto a shop whose only source of air was a window onto the courtyard. The interior of this lair suddenly took on a luxurious tinge thanks to the modern art that decorated the walls. A shaky table, a few worm-eaten benches, and a big smoky lamp gave the room the air of a cave.

Every Wednesday hirsute comrades, their shirts hanging open, and bareheaded corsetless girls in sandals shut themselves in there. The most elevated subjects were dealt with. The speakers were sometimes famous scientists or well-known writers. Life's most serious problems were argued over. And people who came by unexpectedly left amazed that there hadn't been any orgies.

How sometimes one takes for madness what is nothing but scientific reasoning.

Every self-respecting anarchist must live scientifically. His food, his clothing must be reasoned and rational. Some get carried away.

O science, what foolishness is committed in your name!

One summer evening we were waiting on Rue Muller in Montmartre for a speaker, an illustrator at the medical school, who was to talk about hygiene. The hour passed without his appearing. Suddenly, there was a commotion in the crowd near the Sainte-Marie stairway. Five hundred screaming and gesticulating people accompanied a man in bathing trunks. It was our speaker.

"You're crazy, my poor man," said a policeman attracted by the uproar.

"Not at all," the other man said. "I dress in keeping with my ideas. Pores in the skin excreting a harmful substance elaborated by the sweat glands must be free. This is why you see me barely dressed. Those who cover themselves in material in this heat are the ones who are mad."

"So I'm right . . . ," the policeman concluded. "C'mon, time to go to the police station."

The police inspector pretty much shared the opinion of his subordinate. Three doctors were consulted.

"He is healthy of mind," they declared.

The sight of three doctors being in agreement impressed the inspector.

"I'd love to believe you," he said to the men of the healing arts, "but tell your client that if he ever returns to my quarter dressed like that he's going straight to the prison's infirmary for people like him."

A More Practical Science

Another of them, one more practical, applied all his science to not paying his rent. One day I was at his home accompanied by three or four friends. Someone knocked on the door.

"Come in!"

The landlord, flanked by the concierge, blew into the room.

"Monsieur P. . . ."

"That is I."

"I'm here for the rent."

"Excuse me?"

"The rent."

P. seemed to reflect for a moment and made a gesture signifying he didn't understand. Finally, he opened a dictionary and read: "Rent. A tear in an object."

He turned and sternly said to the landlord. "Where is there a tear?"

"Funny guy," said the concierge.

"I must have heard wrong. Wren, a bird. Are you claiming you can fly?"

"I'm claiming nothing but my *rent*."

"Oh, you're the landlord! Why didn't you say so sooner? I'm going to demonstrate as clear as day that property is theft."

"I know, I know," the landlord impatiently said.

"You think you know. Let me explain it to you."

And the speech began. Fifteen minutes later, the landlord, defeated, gave up.

"Forget about him. He's a madman, but an educated one," he said, taking the concierge with him.

Which is exactly the opinion the Count de Guiche had of Cyrano de Bergerac.

Shocking the bourgeois, what a triumph!

These are the little games of anarchy, quite innocent ones, I confess. I still have a pronounced weakness for them. Shocking the bourgeois is such a great pleasure. I once even succeeded in shocking Carouy, who was not precisely a bourgeois.[5] Carouy was very careful with his money; he was even a tad of a tightwad. Any useless expense hurt him more than words can express.

One evening I was out for a stroll with him and Kibalchich on Boulevard Saint-Michel. Our fortune was exactly three francs fifty centimes, and Carouy knew it. Kibalchich gave me a signal, and I distributed all of it to kids we passed on the street. Carouy was literally foaming at the mouth: "You can't possibly be such a sucker!" he said over and over.

The next day the whole anarchist world knew the story, and Carouy told anyone who wanted to hear that Kibalchich and I deserved to starve to death and that anyone who took an interest in us was an idiot. … I'm not a scientist nor am I an illegalist. As I already said, I find the risks of illegalism disproportionate to the results. It's not because there's a tin of sardines missing from a grocery store display window that the face of society will be changed. Nevertheless, I have to admit that certain illegalists didn't lack boldness. A friend of mine, an old, bohemian poet, told me the following story, which he really loved.

One Sunday he was out for a walk with a notorious illegalist on Rue Clignancourt. The poor old man hadn't had lunch the day before; he'd also forgotten to dine.

"Things can't go on like this," the sympathetic illegalist said. "Come with me. I've got an idea."

At the same moment he whistled at his dog. A poultry seller a bit further along was finishing laying out his wares. At a sign from his master the dog leapt, snatched a chicken, and fled. The merchant ran after him. The comrade calmly took a second chicken and put a third in the hands of the confused poet.

"Let's get out of here," he said.

---

5   Edouard Carouy (1883–1913), Belgian-born member of the Bonnot Gang, he committed suicide in prison after being found guilty at the trial of the group. —ed.

He stopped abruptly.

"What a fool I am. I forgot the watercress, good watercress from a spring. So healthy for the body."

And he returned to take two bunches.

"My dog doesn't like it," he explained to his companion as he took him to his home.

The dog was waiting for them at the door.

"I never had so good a big meal in my life," my old poet friend admitted.

Where We Hear an Edifying Tale before Getting to Know Comrade Libertad

I spoke yesterday of an illegalist who liked to share. I knew another who wasn't like that at all. Listen to this simple story.

Two comrades, old, extremist illegalists, Metge and Carouy, had refused what is commonly called "a sure thing."[6] But they'd "worked" separately, the first unaware of the second and vice versa. One of them lived in the suburbs, and the other went to ask for asylum at his home.

"Good day, Carouy. Charmed to see you. But you've come at a bad moment; I'm flat broke," said Metge.

"Just like me," said Carouy.

And both together:

"What a mess!"

Between them they had 10,000 francs. "No matter, stay anyway," the suburban dweller said. "We'll manage." And they managed. That evening, their girlfriends went out into the neighboring fields to pick some cabbages they boiled in water. Not a one of them spent four sous for butter. They were living their lives!

My Best Memories of Anarchism

Having also set out to live my life, my first steps led me to the newspaper *l'anarchie*, which was then edited on Rue du Chevalier-de-la-Barre by comrade Libertad.

---

6 Marius Metge (1890–1933), draft evader and member of the Bonnot Gang, he was sentenced to the penal colony at their trial. —ed.

Libertad's name follows me. It is he who left me my best, my purest memories of anarchy.

It was impossible to look at this man with a mix of pity and amazement. I can still see his enormous head with its bristling beard, topped by long curly hair, his eyes steel blue, piercing and searching, his broad brow, his aquiline nose, his sensuous mouth. All of this atop a stunted, puny body. Only his arms were those of an athlete. Supporting himself on two crutches he moved along with tiny leaps at a harmonious rhythm. Libertad was activity itself: he never missed a brawl.

He was a demonstration in human form, a latent riot.

A member of the Academy, a real one, one day asked comrade Constant to introduce him to Libertad. The "Immortal" wanted to learn about anarchy.[7]

Libertad placed his crutches in a corner and sat down before being asked to do so. He didn't trouble himself with removing his hat, since he never wore one.

"Constant told me you wanted to educate yourself," he said to the stunned academician. "I'm willing to take this on. You're a man of letters, which is something of a bother. I'd have preferred you were a cobbler or a bricklayer. You've got tons of diplomas, which is serious. All the foolishness you've learned prevents you from seeing clearly. I'm going to have to operate on your cataracts."

The academician considered it pointless to continue the conversation.

Libertad's Journey to Glory

Libertad's youth had been a tormented one. Illegitimate son of a prefect, a student at the lycée in Bordeaux, young Albert—Albert and nothing more—one day leapt over the wall and took to the open road.

He headed to Paris, living off charity.

At nightfall, people out strolling late would meet a strange being at the edge of the woods, waving enormous cudgels and

---

7   Members of the Académie Française are known as Immortals. —ed.

demanding charity with so fearsome a voice that people hardly dared refuse him.

One winter night a comrade, who edited *Le Libertaire*, saw a young deformed man shivering on a bench on Boulevard Rochechouart.[8]

"Come with me," he said.

A moment later, the comforted vagabond was sleeping indoors on a pile of newspapers. Young Albert—for it was he—spent a few days at *Le Libertaire*, making himself useful.

"It stinks of a sideshow here," a comrade remarked, about whom it's hard to say if he was more stupid than he was evil.

Albert understood and left.

He left with nothing but a name: Libertad.

Dying of hunger, Libertad went to Sacré Coeur. Bread tickets are distributed there, but you have to hear mass, and after mass the sermon. The priest had hardly spoken a few sentences when a vehement voice called out: "I request the floor." And in the great silence of the church Libertad spoke.

I allow you to imagine what he said. Clamor filled the immense nave. Nothing could calm the orator.

The Swiss Guards and the beadles wanted to grab hold of the madman. Backed up against the pulpit, Libertad waved his crutches so threateningly that they lost all hope of getting close to him. The shocked audience continued to listen to the rebellious speech. Finally, a vicar went to find a piece of cloth and from high on the pulpit let it fall on the head of the stubborn speaker. Wrapped, tied, and rolled up, Libertad was taken to the police station on Rue Dancourt. He served a six-month sentence. He was on his way.

The Abstentionist Candidate

Maimed and crippled, Libertad demonstrated constantly. Dressed in the long black jacket of a typesetter, his hair uncombed, he

---

8   *Le Libertaire* was perhaps the most important of French anarchist newspapers of the period. Edited by Sébastien Faure. —ed.

could be found wherever there was a fight. And what a voice, my friends! He was a leader.

How many times did I see him backed against a wall, handling his crutches like clubs, waving them wildly? No one dared approach him. At moments like these he was truly handsome.

One of his noblest campaigns was the one he carried out in the eleventh arrondissement as an abstentionist candidate. When you demonstrate, the least that can happen to you is that you're arrested. Libertad often was. But there, too, he had his ways.

When he considered all resistance impossible, he would suddenly remember he was infirm. The police would have in their grips nothing but a suffering body, from which an infinite lament emanated.

"You're hurting me, don't touch my leg! Don't touch my arm!"

He was so good at this that after a few arrests, which caused them the greatest bother, the police thought it better never to arrest Libertad.

On the other hand, they mercilessly locked up all those around him. This was all that was needed for certain of our people—whom I have no words for—to accuse Libertad of being a snitch.

Anarchist justice differs little from that of men.

The Strange Life, Death, and Succession of Libertad

Libertad loved public meetings above all else. If there was one in Paris or its suburbs he rushed there on his crutches. He went surrounded by his few but determined supporters. He went to spread the good word. It was dangerous to refuse him the tribune.

It was an evening in Nanterre. There was a great socialist gathering. A deputy was in the chair. He had tightened his ideas, but not his belly, which stuck out. He was as big and round as you could imagine, the joy of all eyes, though perhaps not the mind.

Libertad and his friends entered. They'd forgotten to invite him.

"I demand the floor!" Libertad shouted.

"The meeting is over," the presiding deputy responded.

What followed was epic. The anarchists rushed forward, seizing the desk.

"The meeting will continue!" cried a comrade.

The socialists went on the attack. Blows were exchanged on all sides. Suddenly—an unforgettable spectacle—one could see the people's representative, separated from his voters, lifted, carried, dragged off by unrespecting hands passing him through the window. Alas, not all of him passed through.

The rule that where the head can pass so can the rest wasn't made for him. He was stuck halfway through. All that could be seen was an enormous sphere, tossed by the swell, that Libertad struck, crying with childlike joy: "Move it, tubby, Move it!"

Another memory:

One evening a speaker said to his stunned listeners, not beating about the bush: "Your brains are as filthy as your feet."

A general protest rose.

"Show your feet, come on, show them," he said.

"Show us yours, if you dare," an opposing voice shouted.

With no hesitation, on the tribune, before five hundred people, the orator took off his shoes and waved his naked toes under the public's nose.

"Here are my feet, since you want to see them!"

No one imitated him.

Libertad's Death

Libertad's death was almost as mysterious as his birth. Weakness laid him low from time to time. But he quickly recovered, always as eager and feisty.

As a result of a dispute he was kicked in the stomach. A short time after he took to his bed and was transported to the Lariboisière Hospital. He died there a week later. In his will he'd left his body to the Academy of Medicine. The autopsy revealed that the kick had nothing to do with his premature end, and that death was a result of physical exhaustion.

It perhaps had other causes. Private sorrows tormented that proud mind. Disagreements with formerly faithful friends sharpened his suffering. He felt his life's work growing feeble and veering off course. This man so ferocious, so enraged, who scorned human weakness was, deep down, gentle, sentimental, a dreamer. I saw him cry. "Revolt was not his sole mistress."

He died aged thirty-three.

Libertad's Heirs

The battles that sometimes break out over bourgeois inheritances are child's play compared to those of the anarchists when they think they have interests to defend.

In anarchy, everyone had equal rights. Which, logically, means that no one has any. That's the theory, which I have nothing against. But in practice things are completely different.

The arsenal of anarchist laws is not very complicated. Once again it was demonstrated that "might is right" is the best. However, is that really the case, since taking everything into account, after a few weeks it was Mr. Lorulot who would benefit from all this. As you can imagine, the latter was in no way involved in anything having to do with the passing on of the inheritance. Mr. Lorulot, who is not an illegalist in writing or in speech, is even less so in acts.

The Colonist Lorulot

Like a subprefect, Lorulot likes to stroll in the woods. He doesn't write poetry; he's content with reading it.

This happened a few years ago. He who was to become a well-known individualist militant was at the time nothing but a simple colonist at the communist colony of Saint-Germain. In principle, a communist colony consists in the assembling of a few good men and women who, withdrawing from the greater society, have undertaken the creation of a future society within the greater society of today.

It often begins with an appeal for the solidarity of comrades and almost always ends in squabbles. But Lorulot never does anything like everyone else. He was a peculiar colonist, or, if you prefer, a singular one.

One summer day, on a stifling afternoon, the entire colony was working in order to assure common sustenance. Some were gardening, others were repairing shoes or clothing, others were doing household chores.

"Where's Lorulot?" someone asked.

"Lorulot! Hey Lorulot," they all shouted.

No answer. Worry gripped the colony.

Had some misfortune befallen the excellent comrade? They set out to search for him.

An Elevated Mind

The investigation was lengthy. They scrutinized the thickets, they dug through the copse in the forest. In vain. No Lorulot. They began to lose hope when suddenly a noise echoed.

"Wait a second, I'm not wrong. … Yeah, that's him."

A colonist pointed to the top of a tree. Yes indeed, it was him, peacefully seated on a branch. Mr. Lorulot was reading poetry. He had even adopted a seasonally appropriate costume: he was naked. Naked as a jaybird, or as the day he was born, whichever you prefer.

In chorus, hands around their mouths to magnify their voices, they called out: "Hey, Lorulot." The latter looked down, and the following conversation took place.

"What are you, nuts? What are you doing there?"

"As you can see, I'm bathing."

"You're bathing?"

"Of course, I'm sun bathing."

And, doctrinally: "If you weren't so ignorant, you'd know that anarchists must take sun baths."

But a grump replied: "And while you're doing that, we have to slave away in your place?"

Lorulot took a moment and let drop these definitive words: "Naturally. You are the arms, and so you must work. I am the brain, and so I think."

And he started to read.

Lorulot, incidentally, loved to stroll nude in the forest. He always had the air of a dreamer. What was he seeking? A coconut tree, perhaps.

Lorulot the sociologist had nothing on Lorulot the colonist. Before dedicating himself to oils, he made the banana the key element of the social question. He had this to say to workers: "You are too demanding. If life becomes too dear it's your fault.

Instead of always calling for wage raises wouldn't you do better to eliminate all needs that are not truly necessary? Eliminate meat and fish from your meals. They're superfluous. Be happy with a daily banana. Chemically it's a complete and natural food. No more strikes, no more bosses, no more workers, no more unions, thanks to the banana."

And what was best was that he preached by example. Of course, at that moment he was passing through one of his poor phases.

Anarchy on Oil

Above the arms, the brain. Above the sea, the lighthouse. Above the illegality of action, Mr. André Roulot, alias Lorulot. There's one thing that surprises me, and that's when the prince of thinkers was chosen he wasn't thought of. Mr. Brisset is fine; Lorulot would have been better.[9]

All Mr. Brisset discovered was that man descended from frogs. For his part, Lorulot is ready to demonstrate that he descends from the whale.

The oil this cetacean contains in his flanks is humanity's genitor. Oil is health, oil is life, oil is salvation. It allows birth, life, and preservation.

Even today, when we want to preserve flesh destined for consumption for a few years we hasten to give them an oil bath. Think of sardines in oil, mackerel in oil … Isn't that convincing enough?

It's so obvious that it's confusing.

Mr. Lorulot lives in conformity with his ideas. This apostle of secular and mandatory oleofaction imposes daily consumption of oil on himself. He is preserving himself.

And please don't think I'm making anything up.

In the same way others drink wine, cider, or beer, Mr. Lorulot drinks oil. He drinks it to the health of his theories and to lord only knows what caricature of anarchism. And what is more,

---

9   Jean-Pierre Brisset (1837–1910), pastry chef and thinker who developed eccentric theories concerning language development and humanity's descent from frogs. —ed.

these eccentricities are quite frequent. In Romainville I saw comrades nourishing themselves almost exclusively on grass, like donkeys. In doing so they intended to solve the problem of the dearness of life.

Obviously!

And they added that this food was the only one that was rational, the only one in conformity with the demands of the human organism. They claimed to be disciples of Haeckel and Büchner.

Ever and always science!

Mr. Lorulot likes to compare himself to a lighthouse standing before the sea of people, pointing out the right road to the masses.

His credentials as an oil drinker immediately rendered Mr. Lorulot famous (in our circles, of course). Buried and forgotten, the water drinkers. Some individualists gazed on him with admiring eyes. Something like him had never been seen before. The rice eaters and nature boys were pale figures before this intrepid oil drinker. … Lorulot was crowned leader, and it was a near thing that holy oil weren't poured over him. Everything the man produced was passionately read and commented on.

Youth Is a Beautiful Thing

Let's get a little fresh air.

At *l'anarchie* there were good and devoted comrades.

I knew one of them, the son of a wealthy family. His parents provided him with a generous monthly allowance. He never kept anything for himself and turned everything over to the cause for propaganda purposes. If a poverty-stricken comrade came to see him, he immediately offered him his bed and his room. There were days when the temperature was down in the twenties where he slept in the corridor, exposed to drafts. Always of goodwill, he was always charged with the difficult tasks. The heaviest packages of printed material didn't scare him off, and, even more, he would refuse to take the metro in order to save three sous. One day he came home with a dozen rotten herrings. "I got them for four sous," he said triumphantly. This was his food for a week.

Other rich people, children of the bourgeoisie, carried away by the idea, also provided unlimited sums of money and support.

They were granted the great honor of being admitted to the common table.

"They come to have the filth washed off them," the comrades would say, whose scorn for elementary hygiene was proverbial.

O youth!

Whoever wanted to came to sit at the table. But those who arrived first thought they had certain rights, even if only squatter's rights. And they made this clearly felt. But neither rebuffs nor reproaches nor insults discouraged the guests. You either have a stomach or you don't.

Nevertheless, one of them once got extremely angry. After being given a gold coin, he was sent to go shopping. When he returned he noticed, when he checked the change, that he'd been given a lead piece.

"Damn shopkeeper!"

I never laughed so hard in my life.

I Meet Kibalchich

In Lille on a speaking tour in the North I met a young man with troubling, dark eyes. His mouth was thin and scornful, his hands well kept, his gestures precious. He was wearing a white flannel Russian blouse, embroidered with white silk, inside which a frail chest floated. He spoke with a gentle, caressing voice and chose his words carefully. I found him enormously unpleasant. What a poseur! I said to myself. He said to my friend Mauricius[10]: "Who's the little goose that's with you?"

This was my first encounter with Kibalchich.

Kibalchich had come to Lille in the company of a young woman who, by extraordinary chance, I'd loaned my identity papers to so she could get into Belgium. These are the kinds of services anarchists willingly render each other. This young woman had just been expelled from Belgium for propaganda activity.

The result was an imbroglio that Mr. Gilbert, my examining magistrate, was never able to untangle.

---

10 Pseudonym of Maurice Vandamme (1886–1974), one of the central figures of French anarchist individualism. —ed.

"Strange," that excellent man said. "The reports of the Belgian police speak of the presence of Anna Estorges, wife of Maîtrejean, in Brussels at the same time as the Parisian police reports note your uninterrupted presence at the newspaper *l'anarchie* on Rue du Chevalier-de-la-Barre in Montmartre. Can you explain this to me?"

I didn't do so.

At the criminal trial the prosecution found itself in an awkward position when it tried to explain the simultaneous presence of the same person in two different cities.

Have no fear, Mr. Gilbert: the explanation has now been given.

l'anarchie under Lorulot was definitely not for me, so I set out on a journey. I went to Italy with Mauricius.

"Filthy bourgeois," our good comrades said.

Even so, they didn't dare accuse us of dipping into the newspaper's cash box.

I fell ill in Rome with a cerebrospinal meningitis. I returned to Paris in a different mood from that with which I had departed.

I ran into Kibalchich again. He had gone to Paris shortly after his stay in Lille. He had been rather coldly received at *l'anarchie*. He stunk of the "intellectual," and this was something certain comrades could not excuse. As for me, he got on my nerves more and more with each passing day.

A regular at our Monday talks, he would sometimes take the floor. I would immediately intervene to argue against him, which I did sharply. He responded politely. I could have slapped him.

A mutual friend, who exerted a strong moral influence over me for the past three years, ceaselessly mocked us.

He told me: "All you would need would be to chat for an hour and you'd find yourselves in agreement."

And one fine day he officially introduced us to each other at the people's university of Faubourg Saint-Antoine. My old friend was right.

A Dreamer: Callemin

I saw Kibalchich again the next day at the Luxembourg Gardens. Alone, sad, and distraught, he told me his life's story. He had spent time in Brussels.

"There I met a strange little man named Callemin," he confided in me. "He's a dreamer. In Brussels he'd met a young Russian woman. He loved her with a pure and platonic love. Between them there was only ever an exchange of ideas. The little Russian woman left for Moscow and Callemin was inconsolable. He writes verses and strolls among the stars. He repeats over and over: 'Oh, if only I were handsome; if only I were strong.'"

"Poor kid," Kibalchich concluded.

Every day we met in the Luxembourg Gardens. This was the beginning of a precious and fragile friendship. We both loved poets, twilights, and music. We spent many mornings in the Bois de Boulogne, and many evenings among the docks.

"And to think," Kibalchich said to me, "that I'd briefly thought you a 'scientific.'"

Good god!

Where Carouy and Garnier Make an Appearance

We occasionally went to hear talks.

Like me, Kibalchich had become a declared enemy of illegalism. If he had briefly accepted it in theory, he condemned it strongly in practice, given its pitiful results.

Mr. Lorulot gave a talk in late 1911. We attended it.

Illegalism was on the order of the day. Mr. Lorulot maintained a prudent silence on the subject, and it must be noted that this great man never wrote a word or spoke in public on this burning question.

For his part, Kibalchich spoke his mind. He said to the sardine thieves: "You're all idiots."

"Sellout! Traitor!" a voice shouted.

It was Carouy.

A threatening fist was waved, that of Garnier.

There was quite a ruckus. For a second I had a clear feeling that we were going to have our faces smashed in without a word of discussion.

Among the most violent could be found a few of the comrades who would later be our companions at the criminal trial.

Which didn't prevent certain anarchists from declaring at the trial that our anti-illegalism was of too fresh a date to be sincere and that it was simply a way for us to save our hides.

Mr. Lorulot, called as a witness, didn't remember.

Kibalchich received a letter from Callemin. Clearly Belgium wasn't kind to the bashful lover. The administrative commission of the Maison du Peuple in Brussels had just forbidden him access to the building.

"No anarchists here!" they'd told him.

"I'm too much for them," he wrote.

At the Luxembourg Gardens Kibalchich introduced me to a very gentle, very timid, very quiet young man.

You had to tear his words from him, but little by little he grew animated. He quoted tirades of Anatole France's from memory and recited quite beautifully poems by Jehan Rictus.[11] If you pushed him a bit you could see he's educated: he had read and retained much.

His mask was pained and brutal. Involuntarily I thought of Poil de carotte.[12]

"Au revoir, Valet," Kibalchich said, when the young man left us.[13]

Still at the Luxembourg Gardens, we meet a counterfeiter. He's disillusioned. Professionally, things are going poorly for him. Middlemen are ruining him. Everyone wants a small commission. The purchase of primary materials is costly.

---

11 Jehan Rictus (1867–1933), pseudonym of Gabriel Randon de Saint-Amand, a poet who wrote in the language of the Parisian streets. —ed.

12 Titular character of the novel of a difficult childhood by Jules Renard. —ed.

13 René Valet (1890–1912), locksmith and illegalist anarchist. Killed by the police in a battle in Nogent-sur-Marne. —ed.

Working fifteen hours a day, he hardly makes three francs. He judges harshly those who fence and spend the fake money.

"They're all thieves," he says.

The Anarchist Baron

When I met Kibalchich I was broke, and he was scarcely wealthier than I. But he had a friend, a doctor of philosophy, who offered us lodging.

It was on Rue Tournefort, the top floor of a building, a large attic room. There was a window, but it was a little high. In order to get some air I was forced to climb on a table. But what a beautiful view! We looked down on a large garden planted with tall fruit trees. In the middle was a beautiful well of wrought iron. And in the back was a house where Balzac had lived for a long time.

The room was plastered with lime. The main piece of furniture was a large samovar brought there by Kibalchich. And while we drank tea our host ate hashish or drank ether.

He was the kind of philosopher we don't often see.

He had a student, a young man of seventeen, an authentic baron, Mr. de Ch …

How was it that chance led the family of this young man to entrust his education to such a professor? This was something Kibalchich and I were never able to understand. And God knows that we were broad minded!

But anyway, blessed was the student, for he brought his teacher two hundred francs monthly. Our arrival didn't disrupt classes. On the contrary.

"I was bored at the high school," the young baron said. "Here I have fun."

"I've got good news for you," he one day said to Kibalchich. "I convinced my father to allow me to take lessons in style, and you'll be the professor."

It was too good to be true. It couldn't last. Vacation time came. The young candidate was dismissed and everything came crashing down.

Valet Declaims Poetry

It was a good period. With the baron gone all we were lacking was money, something to which we didn't attach great importance. And in any event, we had friends. Valet came to see us. He loved to talk literature and recite poetry. I remember an evening when, lacking oil, we lit a candle. In the trembling flame, Valet's pained mask took on an expression of extraordinary suffering, and with a disconsolate voice he spoke of sad, so sad things. …

Carouy's Coin

One day the visit of Carouy, whom Kibalchich had known in Brussels but who I'd never met, was announced.

"He's come to kill you," my friend was told.

"Damn," Kibalchich said. "He's the kind of man to do just that. But what's he got against me?"

"You swindled him."

"That would be all the more stupid since Carouy isn't someone you try to pull a swindle on. Anyway, let him in. We'll hash it out."

And Carouy came in, accompanied by a mutual friend.

Kibalchich was slightly on his guard. But his distrust quickly faded, for Carouy had such a nice smile.

"I'll eat with you with no fuss, whatever you're having is fine," he said.

Kibalchich looked at me worriedly: we didn't have ten sous between us. The mutual friend understood the look.

"Come on," he said to Carouy. "We'll go shopping."

It was a charming lunch, and as he left Carouy offered Kibalchich a louis.

"Take it, my good man. That would make me happy."

And he added, enigmatically: "I'm leaving tonight on a trip and it will bring me luck."

Kibalchich said to me, showing me the twenty-franc piece: "You see this louis? Well, it's the most extraordinary thing I've seen in all my life, since Carouy isn't very generous."

The next day we ran into Carouy.

"Back already?"

"An amazing trip."

There are no crooked schemes like those in anarchy.

As soon as he arrived in Paris the young baron de Ch … , though raised in the best principles, had not disdained resorting to a tiny stratagem aimed at notably increasing the monthly allowance sent him by his father in the provinces.

The student was boarding at the luxuriously furnished home of an individual on Boulevard Arago. For 500 francs a month lodgers were housed, fed, and had their laundry done.

"Can you be kind enough to mark up the bill a little?" he asked his host.

The latter didn't need to be asked twice.

Two straight months he sent his father the baron bills for 800 francs. The young baron dedicated the 300 supplementary francs to raucous feasts.

"What a nice guy my host is," he would say.

He changed his mind the day when, trying to enter his room, he found the doors sealed. An investigating magistrate had been by.

Too late, alas, for the accommodating host, who was being sought for all kinds of swindles, had fled, taking with him the linens and wardrobe of his young tenant.

Is a bourgeois swindle any better than an anarchist swindle?

Soudy's Jinx

I met Soudy in a bar in the Latin Quarter frequented by anarchists.[14]

He was introduced to me as a good comrade, already sentenced twice for resisting arrest. He had never had any luck.

At eleven he was already working at a grocery. Affiliated with the grocery union, he had first received a one-month, then a three-month sentence for distribution of tracts in front of large grocery stores during a strike.

---

14 André Soudy (1892–1913), member of the Bonnot Gang who came to be known as the "Man with the Rifle," which he carried and aimed during holdups. —ed.

He constantly said, "What do you expect? I'm jinxed. I always get stuck taking the fall."

He said this with the tone of a resigned Pierrot. He came to see us often on Rue Tournefort. He gradually confided in me. He'd lived with a cousin for two years whom he adored madly. She left him. … A year later, he ran into her in Montmartre. The idyll picked up where it had left off, but ended quickly. Soudy was admitted to Saint-Louis Hospital, seriously ill, but cured of many illusions.

Jinxed, Forever Jinxed

Before being admitted to the hospital he had entrusted the keys to his room to a friend.

"You can use it while I'm away," he told him. "I'll be gone for some time."

One day the friend was arrested. He had stolen a postman's bicycle. When the police inspector asked for his address, he gave Soudy's. A search. At first, they found (of course) tins of sardines, and then, much more serious, a bunch of skeleton keys and a jimmy.

His friends grew worried and tried to kidnap him from the hospital. In order to do so, they gave some money to a comrade. The comrade wasted the money. Soudy was transferred to La Santé Prison. Not receiving any care, he left with tuberculosis.

His eternal bad luck!

A Tiny Illegalist

With all that, he wasn't a bad person. All he could be attacked for was an unfortunate penchant for schemes. But he was only a tiny illegalist. He often came to see us on Rue Fessart.

His greatest pleasure was to go out for a walk with my two little girls and little Dieudonné, who was en pension with us at the time.[15] He was very attentive to them. Knowing himself

---

15 Eugène Dieudonné (1884–1944), falsely accused of being a member of the Bonnot Gang, he was nevertheless sentenced to forced labor, escaped, and finally pardoned thanks to the efforts of journalist Albert Londres. —ed.

condemned, he was careful, whenever he bought them pastry, to have them served directly by the shopkeeper. The children adored him. His arrival was greeted with shrieks of joy.

"The Bécamelle is here! The Bécamelle is here!" they'd sing in chorus.

The little grocer laughed heartily.

He was always ready to make himself useful. His friends showed no discretion in hitting him up: he was unable to refuse them.

Three days after his arrest I learned in Saint-Lazare about the Chantilly Affair, but my shock was great when I learned of the role Soudy had played in it.[16]

I couldn't imagine little Bécamelle with a rifle firing on passersby. It's true he missed them all and as soon as he got in the car he fainted. How could he have allowed himself to get involved in that mess?

I don't know anything about it, but everything leads me to believe that it was yet another service he was asked to render and that he didn't dare refuse.

* * *

I barely knew Bonnot. He was from the provinces. All I remember of him is this one thing.

Platano was his only friend. One day, Platano inherited 27,000 francs.

"Let's band together," he said to Bonnot. "We'll found a business."

"Gladly," Bonnot replied.

With which they both set for Paris, in a car that incidentally was stolen.

The game warden of Lieusaint found on the road a man gasping for breath with several pistol wounds; the man died in his arms. It was Platano. Arriving alone in Paris, Bonnot explained

---

16 Chantilly is the site of the bank where the Bonnot Gang carried out its last holdup on March 25, 1912. Two employees were killed, and the gang escaped with 47,555 francs. —ed.

to his friends that Platano injured himself while handling a Browning.

"It was too compromising to take care of him," he added, "so I finished him off."

Did he have the right to do so?

Lengthy discussions on the topic were held among the illegalists, one, it must be said, that was totally platonic.

When Bonnot's mistress's home in Lyon was later searched, twenty-seven 1,000-franc bills were found under the floorboards—a simple coincidence, the Bonnotists asserted—exactly the amount Platano is supposed to have had on him at the moment of his death.

A Country Outing

Louise Dieudonné invites me to go to Romainville.

"Come early," she wrote. "We'll go by bicycle."

At exactly 5:00 a.m. I knocked on the door of the house on Rue de Bagnolet. Carouy, Garnier, and Callemin were already ready to leave. Louise Dieudonné and Marie Vuillemin hadn't yet arrived.

"Oh women!" Callemin grumbled. "They really complicate life."

Finally, all six of us set off on our bikes. At the Porte de Romainville Marie Vuillemin's tire gave up the ghost. Garnier rushed over and started to fix it. Guillemin was beside himself:

"Let her figure it out herself," he told his friend. "She's nothing but a bother."

The Vuillemin woman protested. An insane rage gripped Raymond-la-Science and, turning to Garnier, still kneeling before the bike: "Octave," he implored, "please give me permission to kick him in the . . ."

The tire repaired, we set out. We reached Nogent.

"Shall we go canoeing?"

"Gladly," the two men responded.

In the anarchist world it's rare that women are asked their opinion.

Carouy in Love

We untied a large boat. I settled myself at the helm with Louise Dieudonné. Callemin lay down in the bottom of the boat, at our feet. Carouy and Garnier took the oars and Marie Vuillemin, still pouting, sat at the other end. The weather was overcast but mild. Heavy clouds rushed across the sky. The languid countryside had trouble awakening. Both of them being robust, Carouy and Garner rowed vigorously.

The boat glided over the water. Cool and perfumed air caressed our faces. I felt like I was a little schoolgirl. A kind of tenderness seemed to have swept over Callemin. He raised to Louise Dieudonné and me eyes that were anything but evil. My word, he was becoming languorous.

It was all so extraordinary that Louise and I broke out in laughter. But Carouy stopped abruptly. His oars hung in the air.

"Sing something for us, Louise" he asked,

Louise was the beautiful voice of the society.

"What do you want me to sing," she answered.

"A romance," responded Carouy, who had a weakness for sentimental compositions.

The boat floated with the tide; the singer's voice climbed into the air:

> The air is full of songs
> And loving things,
> The hedges and bushes
> Are all covered in roses
> The joyful nightingale
> Sing on each branch
> For every lover,
> Today is Sunday.

It was Carouy's song, and with his deep voice, he picked up the chorus:

> Gay nightingale in your joyous songs
> Beneath the blue sky, sing of victorious love.

But don't approach lovers.
For this is how I lost my heart.

Carouy was enchanted: he sang "my heart" with a quivering voice. Garnier too sang a couplet. It was an idyllic and charming morning. Callemin absentmindedly plucked waterlilies that the boat brushed against and made a bouquet of them. There was a bistro on the banks. We docked. While the hostess laid the plates, we strolled arm in arm. We followed a shady road along the viaduct. Small houses, small huts buried in the greenery followed one after the other.

"It's charming around here," said Carouy, humming the tune "It's Here I'd Like to Live."

It was precisely there that he would die.

The stroll sharpened our appetites. We stuffed ourselves on café au lait, cakes, and croissants. We looked like a gang of high schoolers on the loose.

In the trees the birds were singing. A starry bud trembled at the end of each branch. The sun finally rose. The sentimental Carouy tried to yodel.

"Life is good," Garnier said.

But Callemin was incapable of letting a remark pass without melting it in his scientific crucible.

"Excuse me . . . ," he began.

Carouy didn't give him the time to continue.

"Shut up," he simply said.

Temptations and Hesitations

In the meanwhile, in Lorulot's hands the newspaper *l'anarchie* was hardly prospering. Lorulot expressed his intention to leave it.

People pressured Kibalchich and me to take over for him. "Not on your life," I shouted. "I just got over the last time." I still felt the effects of the few weeks I'd spent after Libertad's death on Rue du Chevalier-de-la-Barre alongside Mauricius.

I recalled the endless attacks we suffered. Not for anything in the world did I want to start up a life like that again.

I said to Kibalchich: "Think about it, my friend. We'll be surrounded by illegalists. The water is rising so quickly that neither you nor I will be able to dam it. We'll be submerged in no time."

I reminded him of the already-ancient talks where Garnier and Bonnot had threatened to beat us up.

Kibalchich listened to me with a smile. He had the gentle and polite stubbornness of a Slav. And what is more, he didn't fear blows.

He said over and over: "There's work to be done ... There's work to be done ... There's work to be done. Believe me and accept."

I ended up giving in, nevertheless imposing a condition: that we not be charged with the financial end of the paper.

Lorulot was perfect. He went along with all our wishes. Perhaps he was in a hurry to leave ...

"Who's staying behind to look after the cash box?" I asked him.

He answered, "Callemin."

The latter, incidentally, during the little time he remained in that post, was a model treasurer.

In Romainville Callemin was not only the cashier; he was also an occasional typesetter. And a strange one.

During the three weeks he spent in our company in Romainville he had to compose an article of Lorulot's. The article notably included this sentence: "Smokers, opiomaniacs, morphinomaniacs, and Baudelairians are all idiots."

My gaze fell on this passage.

"Have you read Baudelaire?" I asked Lorulot.

"Never in my life!" he answered. "I don't have any time to waste."

"So you condemn an author without having read him."

"You know what? You might be right. I'll take back the word 'Baudelairian.'"

He went to the typesetter to make the correction. The paper came out and what did I find among those anathematized but the "Baudelairians."

"Why didn't you remove the word?" I asked Callemin.

"Because it's not Lorulot's opinion, but mine," Callemin answered in a tone that didn't admit of any reply.

We Join l'anarchie

The die was cast. Kibalchich and I entered the newspaper *l'anarchie*. Its offices were no longer on Rue du Chevalier-de-la-Barre: Lorulot had transferred the offices to Rue de Bagnolet in Romainville. He showed us around the house. First a large garden planted with trees and lilacs. A three-story building with a cellar. On the third floor a bedroom where friends passing through could sleep and another room occupied by the convict Huc.

A little further on a second building, composed of a large room where the printing press was kept, a storage shed filled with unsold papers, and a large shower room. On the second floor a bedroom occupied by Garnier. Behind it, a farmyard and then three vegetable gardens that Huc, the convict, cultivated with love.

"I bid you welcome," Lorulot said to us.

And directly addressing me: "Rirette, go cook us something. We'll have lunch together."

On the menu, green beans picked in the garden. I cooked them, adding a touch of vinegar.

Neither Salt nor Pepper

Everyone agreed it was excellent.

"Well, it was anything but in keeping with the Idea," exclaimed Louise Dieudonné at the end of the meal. "You wouldn't have eaten it so heartily had you known Rirette had added a little bit of vinegar."

"She put in vinegar!" roared Callemin.

"She had the nerve to do that!" grumbled Garnier.

"That absolutely takes the cake!" sobbed Carouy.

For a moment I didn't know what was stronger among them, consternation or anger. They had the appalled looks of a priest who by trickery has been made to eat meat on Good Friday. Callemin went so far as to speak of making himself vomit. There was only the convict, Huc, who said nothing.

They finally had the goodness to explain to me that vinegar is an antiscientific food. Only oil is allowed, and I was initiated in Lorulotist cuisine. The list of permitted foods is edifying: corn gruel, puree with milk, peeled vegetables, macaroni and cheese, herb tea (a lot of herb tea), and sugar (of which ten kilograms were used weekly).

"No salt!" Lorulot concluded.

"Or pepper!" Callemin insisted. "It's a stimulant."

"Or chervil," said Garnier. "It's an aphrodisiac."

None of this discouraged Kibalchich.

"You still want to join in with them?" I asked as we were leaving.

"More than ever," he answered.

And so there we were, settled in. Lorulot hung around to bring us up to date. But eating together, which had gone on for a year, was all over. Everyone now ate at home or at little tables in the garden. And it was clear that the comrades could not stomach Kibalchich the intellectual.

When we ate, just the two of us, in the kitchen, we constantly heard the same phrase: "They'd better toe the line or we'll drive them out with pistol blow."

Kibalchich never stopped smiling. Only one thing bothered him: he couldn't get used to the Lorulotic diet. He asked for tea and coffee. It was contrary to all principles. It didn't matter, I made them for him.

Something strange. Every evening that I left a full coffee or tea pot in the kitchen I would invariably find them empty the next morning.

Lorulot Looks On

Things settled down, each working away at his task. Callemin took care of the cash box. Valet set the type. Garnier and Carouy worked the machine by hand. Huc gardened. Kibalchich wrote articles. And Lorulot looked on.

There were, even so, from time to time some blowups. One day Garnier became enraged because an article he wrote called "Salt Is Poison" was refused. He even said, "Anarchy will be scientific or it will not be." But he soon calmed down and put his pistol back in his pocket.

At *l'anarchie* everyone received the same wage, and all the collaborators were equals. Everyone had a right to lodging, food, and laundry.

As for money, there wasn't a sou. If you wanted some, even if it was to purchase clothing or linens, you had to shift for yourself. Kibalchich and I, in order to get by, did some translation work for Povolezky.

Several Disappearances

One fine day, two weeks after our arrival, we learned from the newspapers that a robbery had taken place in the area. Two men, Camburlier and Rogasse, were arrested. They accused Carouy of having been their accomplice. Was this true? Wasn't it? Carouy, who was horrified by prison, even if only held temporarily for questioning, hastily left Romainville.

Two days later his female companion came to move his furniture. We would only see Carouy again in court.

A week later a large-scale departure. Callemin, Garnier, Valet, and Lorulot left us. Callemin handed all the accounts so faithfully kept to a comrade. Not a cent was missing.

Huc continued his gardening.

In Which Balaoo Appears.

We received visitors. There was a perpetual parade of copy bearers.

I remember one of them. A large, square head, beardless, the nose bearing a pair of glasses, a stocky and redoubtable body. On anarchist strolls we would meet him half nude, a tree trunk in his hand, playing at the man of the woods. He had a style of his own and hated shopkeepers and concierges.

Astounding phrases spurted from his pen, like: "Because I often fail to decorate my skull with an incoherent felt cupola reprobation reigns on the face of my doorman."

"We all have our dignity, as many grocers say, and I don't want anyone to take me for an honest man. This is why I gladly consider myself a magnanimous and smiling delinquent, a subhuman scoundrel."

With all that, he was a good man and an impeccable postal employee.

We also had Balaoo.

But this Balaoo ... pitiful, degenerate.

What unforeseen set of circumstances had led this man with his loud laugh, his oblong skull, his disproportionately long arms, his legs always folded in an elastic step to end up among us? An unsolved mystery.

What's most certain is that he came there and intended to return there. His sole eccentricity consisted in dressing in a heavy overcoat in summer and a canvas jacket in winter. He had taken on a vague illegalist tint from having attended meetings. One day he swiped a box of prunes.

"How'd you do it?" we asked him.

"With my hands and feet."

That was Balaoo.

And then there passes through my saddened memory the tall, haughty figure of E.P.

Invariably dressed in a frock coat that reached his feet, he took pride in never making any concessions to what he called "abominable prejudices." His motto was "I submit to nothing and no one."

He died of hunger in Switzerland.

The Repentant Water Drinkers

Callemin, Valet, Garnier, and Carouy having left, they were immediately replaced by other comrades. An anarchist newspaper resembles a mill: whoever wants to enters. It is especially bums who enter, who impose themselves and are not the least bothersome or the least compromising of tenants.

They're never asked where they came from or where they were going. The mania that several of them had of leaving at your house packages for you to hold onto is at the very least strange. These are people who "make do," and when you make do it's always at someone else's expense. Lorulot left, taking with him his recipes. All in all, we preferred the water drinkers we'd encountered on Rue du Chevalier-de-la-Barre, even more because they sometimes were not lacking in imagination.

Weakened by a hemorrhage, laid up in bed, I received a gracious gift from a friend: six bottles of old Médoc.

"This'll get you back on your feet," he said.

I drank a glass. I drank a second. When I went to pour myself a third, I noticed that the six bottles were empty.

The water drinkers had been by.

A Story of Religious Herb Tea

The gardener Huc told me a good story. It was during the good old days in Romainvile. At the common table every day could be found Lorulot and Louise Dieudonné, Carouy and the Belardy woman, Garnier and the Vuillemin woman, and Callemin on his own. The herb tea of the nuns flowed freely. Marie Vuillemin, one day not feeling well, went to the doctor. A long examination.

"What do you drink?" asked the doctor.

"Herb tea."

She gave the name.

"Bring me a bottle of it," said the doctor.

And he analyzed the contents.

The next day the Vuillemin woman returned and learned with shock that the famous herb tea contained a product capable of deranging the most robust of intestines. Drinking it opened the doors wide to enteritis. When this scientific news became known on Rue de Bagnolet the consternation was general.

Good God, who could be trusted? Who could be trusted?

It was replaced by another one, every bit as religious, incidentally.

"This one is fine," the apostle declared.

His disciples believed him.

A Subject of Conversation

It became a mania. All day long at *l'anarchie* the only word that could be heard being conjugated was the verb *bouziller*.

"I'm gonna fuck him up … You're going to fuck me up … he's going to fuck him up … We're going to fuck ourselves up."

Bouziller is a very simple verb, which, in anarchist language, means: lodge a pistol bullet in someone's skin.

In fact, though, no one ever gets fucked up. From time to time one can hear some dry explosions. Fret not: they're firing at a target. Among themselves anarchists are sparing of their bullets.

I can only think of one among us who passed from words to acts, Lacombe.

But then again, he was a madman.

The Unpublished Talk

The postal employee had just brought us a new article. His hatred of shopkeepers and concierges was keeping him awake at night.

"And you, wicked shopkeeper, so laughable, potbellied both physically and intellectually, you sell string beans and nauseating desires to unsuspecting three-year-olds. You're just like an eccentric concierge, like a gaslight."

He pulls me aside.

"I've prepared a talk that I expect will be a great success."

No one had ever spoken on the subject. He declaimed lyrically: "Just as we absorb healthy and appetizing nourishment and expel the superfluous after a few chemical operations, in the same way we fill the courtyard with the splendor of the world and excrete this splendor in the form of art."

And then, having pulled out his watch: "Damn," he said, "I have to hurry, I'm going to reach my office late."

l'anarchie *in Decline*

l'anarchie was doing increasingly poorly. The losses were drowning us. Even more, we were selling hardly any books and pamphlets, and the bookstore had always been the newspaper's principal source of revenue. We had to think things over.

One resource was left us: we had to return to Paris. Still today I wonder why we moved the offices to the suburbs.

Formally saying we were leaving was out of the question: Lorulot had forgotten to tell us in whose name the offices in Romainville were taken.

In any event, it wasn't his. Which didn't prevent us, one fine night, from moving. We had spent exactly three months in Romainville.

I rented something in Paris at 24 Rue Fessart in my own name. The new home of *l'anarchie* consisted of a lodging on the second floor. You entered through the dining room, which also served

as an office. Following it, in a row, there was the inevitable gues-
troom, then at the end our bedroom. There was a series of mini-
gardens, as there are in Belleville, and at the back a storage shed
in which we set up the typesetting machine.

The comrade who had succeeded Callemin as treasurer admitted to us that the cash box was empty. We sold the press and the
paper still came out.

At the request of the comrades I put my name on the front
page. It was I who would henceforth receive all the correspondence. Settled in on Rue Fessart, we no longer saw any of those
who would later make up what has come to be called "the Tragic
Gang," aside from Soudy and Mertge.

What would they have come among us for? Kibalchich's ideas
were in opposition to theirs. The latter was beginning to campaign against illegalism.

Another circle had been formed in Paris, *L'Idée Libre*. They
were far more comfortably set up than we were. There could also
be found the books and pamphlets people might need. They were
also frequently at Ducret's. We ran into them from time to time
at talks and meetings, but that was about all.

This quasi-separation, which had occurred three weeks after
our arrival in Romainville, did not displease us.

"We'll finally be able to do some useful work," the stubborn
Kibalchich repeated over and over. "There are things to do,
things to do."

And he dreamed of an anarchy made of love as much as of
reason, where a place would be reserved for feelings and from
which stupid, idiotic, narrow-minded "scientism," which turns
its believers into individuals ready for any eccentricity and folly,
would be banished.

"They'll end up in the slammer," he would say.

He didn't yet think of the guillotine.

Three Days after the Crime on Rue Ordener. Their Visit

A crime had just been committed on Rue Ordener.[17] Its signature was clear: it was an anarchist crime, or rather a crime of illegalist extremists.

Kibalchich and I looked at each other. Our eyes had the same silent question. Who? Kibalchich let fall a name. I cried out.

"He's crazy enough to have done it," Kibalchich asserted.

In any case, he wasn't alone. We tied to guess who the others were.

"Let's wait and see," I said.

One day passed, two without anything clarifying things in our minds.

At the end of the third day, at 9:00 p.m., someone was scratching at our dining room door, which opened directly onto the landing. It was a tiny, humble scratching, nearly embarrassed. We were alone, having put my two daughters, Maud and Chinette, to bed at 8:00. They were already asleep. The scratching was followed by three knocks. Who were these timid visitors? What a strange way to announce yourself in a house that was so welcoming.

"Go open up," Kibalchich said to me.

I nervously went over to the door. I quickly pulled at the lock and opened the door wide.

We cried in unison: "Them! It's them!"

In the doorway two silhouettes stood out, one tiny the other bigger: it was Callemin and Garnier.

I can still see these two silhouettes. I see them both, doleful, worn down, exhausted. They smelled of discouragement, flight, and confusion. Their new clothes were already crumpled, their shoes dusty. Them! It was they who had done the deed! No doubt was possible.

"Come in," Kibalchich told them in his gentlest voice.

They entered.

"Don't stand there in the dining room," I said. "Anyone coming in could take us by surprise."

---

17 Site of the bank held up by the Bonnot Gang on December 21, 1911. This was the first time a car was used as a getaway vehicle in France. —ed.

"She's right," said Kibalchich.

And, a lamp in his hand, he led our two visitors to the other end of the apartment, to our bedroom. It was a large, rectangular room furnished with a bed in the middle, a folding bed, a chaise lounge, a desk, a bookcase, and a washstand. In the vases, in the cups pretty much everywhere, there were dying flowers. A fire blazed in the fireplace. The purple lampshade emitted a soft light.

"It's nice here," Garnier said as he came in.

"Shhh," Kibalchich said, and he pointed at my two little girls, sleeping peacefully on their folding bed.

"Ahh . . . ," Garnier said.

The two men carefully removed their half-belt overcoats and their hats.

I sat on the foot of the bed, Callemin on the chaise lounge, Garnier on the foot of the children's bed, and Kibalchich on a chair at his desk.

Callemin and Garnier, elbows on their knees, hands crossed, bent over, seemed to be deep in thought. What were they thinking of? Nothing, perhaps. Simply resting their aching bones. A long silence. Kibalchich broke it first.

"So here you are, back from Dieppe."

"Yes," said Callemin, with a tight smile.

His pince-nez were foggy; he wiped them with his handkerchief.

"So it was you."

"Yes," said a somber Garnier.

With a soft voice, muffled so as not to wake the girls, Raymond-la-Science began:

"We've led a horrible life for the past three days. We didn't want to go to our pals' house so as not to compromise them. We're at the end of our rope."

Raymond inspired pity. His haughtiness, his arrogance had abandoned him. He looked like a little child seeking comfort, assistance, and protection. Garnier, withdrawn, said nothing.

"You must be hungry. You want something to eat?"

"No, but I'd like some tea," said Callemin.

"And me some coffee," Garnier said.

The two drinks were prepared. Walking softly, I served the cups. They savored them slowly.

Though gripped by fear—the house, we knew, was surrounded by police—Kibalchich tried to seem happy.

"Well then Raymond, and you, Octave, you're beginning to compromise your principles. One of you is drinking tea and the other coffee. Believe you me, you'll be making other compromises to your scientism."

"If we're allowed the time," answered Callemin, his face growing somber.

"What a stupid story," Garnier continued, seeming to follow an idée fixe. "We had set out on another thing, one that was as easy as could be."

"Unfortunately, it failed. Bonnot said: 'Goddammit, we're not going to go home empty-handed,' and he drove us to Rue Ordener. He had had a tip, He'd planned it all out."

Callemin continued: "There were four of us in the car, but there was one who'd never have come had he known it would involve killing someone."

And Garnier, enraged: "The savage crowd, that ferocious crowd that chased after us. What could it possibly matter to all those imbeciles that we 'explain ourselves' to a messenger? If I could have, I would have killed a quarter of them."

Kibalchich seemed to be in a dream state. Suddenly, he lifted his head and asked, sadly: "How did you come to this?"

"We'd had enough," Callemin answered. "We couldn't go on living the way we did. We had enough of theories, of principles, of axioms. We'd waited long enough for the promised well-being. We thought we'd conquer it all at one go."

He said this dolefully, with a voice that expressed a suffering seeking consolation. He struck me as a child seeking to be lulled. At that moment, he was unquestionably unhappy. Even more because the holdup on Rue Ordener was a pitiful fiasco.

"Everything must be started up anew," Garnier murmured.

"If they give us the time … ," Callemin said again.

A worry gnawed at me.

"Why'd you come here? You know that the house is tightly watched over. You're deliberately throwing yourself from the frying pan into the fire."

"What difference does it make?" Callemin answered. "A little bit sooner, a little bit later . . ."

"The past two days we've felt we were being hunted down, pursued. I have two flaws that make me stand out: my pince-nez and my shortness. I can't do anything about one or change the other. As for Octave, there are his eyes." (Garnier had extraordinarily sparkling eyes.)

"When we walk down the street, I constantly tell him, 'Lower your eyes, Octave ... Octave, lower your eyes.'"

"And I can't grow. There's no avoiding it: we're going to be caught. Look; we haven't even bothered disguising ourselves."

He was right. Both were exactly as they are. Only an enormous exhaustion made their faces drawn.

Through all of this, my two little girls continued to sleep. We could hear their soft, rhythmic breathing. Kibalchich and I were seized with great pity for those two sinister kids who were nothing but two unfortunates.

One o'clock sounded at the church in Belleville.

"Already," Garnier said. "Let's go, Raymond. Time to get moving."

As if reluctantly, they stood up. They wearily put their coats on, put on their bowlers. Callemin adjusted his pince-nez. And both of them, eyes on the alert, hands in their pockets, left. We saw them disappear around the corner of Rue Mélingue. I heaved a sigh of relief. Calm, almost smiling, Kibalchich turned to me.

"You didn't want to admit that Raymond's scientism was all for show? Now do you believe me?"

And, suddenly serious: "I feel like Callemin came here seeking a tiny memory of his adolescence, a time when he, sentimental and dreamy, strolled the streets of Brussels with me."

A Legend

A legend continues to circulate, one that makes the Tragic Bandits the holdup men at two shops where they found arms and ammunition. Nothing could be less true. Callemin, Garnier, and Bonnot never robbed a gun shop. Others took care of that. They came to us to present their merchandise.

They said: "We're salesmen in a bit of a bind. You would do us the greatest favor if you'd buy some 'samples' from us."

I purchased revolvers for Kibalchich and me, paying top dollar. This acquisition would cost us more dearly than I could have imagined. It cost me a year in a holding cell, and as for Kibalchich, well, he's still paying …

I later learned that Callemin, Garnier, and Bonnot had been seduced by the high quality of the weapons. Unfortunately, they didn't have enough money to buy them.

"Not a problem," the accommodating salesmen said. "You'll pay for them when you next have the money in hand."

Buying on credit slightly increases the price, and these intermediaries were paid to the last cent. There are people who know how to get by.

Which can't be said about either Garnier or Callemin.

The Search

The Belardy woman, Carouy's companion, was arrested. She was released a month later on parole. We took her in. She settled herself in on Rue Fessart. It was clear she was being followed. They hoped to get to Carouy through her.

It became difficult to live together, given that Belardy took advantage of the situation. Her friends had a hard time preventing her from committing foolish acts.

One day there was a knock at our door. Sixty agents came in to carry out a search. It was inevitable. Among them, only one thought it his duty to be brutal, an officer, by the way. Mr. Jouin eventually arrived. It was my first encounter with him, and he showed himself to be a gentleman.

That very evening Kibalchich was sent to jail.

Fundraising

Once again Soudy had had rotten luck. The night before the search he had slept in our house in the room of a typesetter who was out working. At 4:00 in the morning he left. Forbidden a residence permit, he feared the arrival of the police, which we sensed was imminent.

"What luck I had," he told me that evening when he learned what had happened. "Had I remained another half hour I was done for."

His fate was to go to Chantilly.

Bonnot, Garnier, Callemin, and Carouy were being mercilessly hunted down. They finally appealed to their pals. They encountered people of goodwill, but their lives were wretched. Certain "comrades," sensing they were being followed, no longer dared return home. Hunger reigned. Bonnot passed forty hours without tasting a morsel of food. The situation was more or less the same for Callemin and Garnier. The three of them remained glued to each other.

"What a god-awful life!" Garner said over and over.

"We can't even try to pull off the least little job," Callemin lamented.

The fact is that they remained in hiding. News got around that they were short of funds. A friend sacrificed himself and took up a collection, which brought in 60 francs.

"I'll bring it to them," someone said.

Everyone admired his courage: this meant running a big risk. Two days later we saw him again. "Well?" we asked.

"They refuse to accept anything," he said. "We can't give anything to *l'anarchie* but can't accept anything from it."

"So give the money back."

"Here's what's left," he said, spreading out six 100-sous coins.

"I spent the other thirty francs," the messenger admitted.

And he held out a bill.

A lovely example of individualism. Do I have to say, to remove any ambiguity, that among communists, where I have many good friends, they don't lower themselves to schemes like these and they repudiate all proceedings euphemistically called illegalism by those who profit from them?

"Loan me some books," the same comrade said.

"Go ahead, choose."

I opened the library. Was it by chance that he chose the newest, least damaged books? He took seventeen. *Numero deus impare gaudet* I would later learn at Saint-Lazare when the chaplain set himself to teaching me Latin.[18]

What to take all these books away in? A tablecloth was on the table, a brand new one. It cost me eighteen francs.

He piled the books up in it.

I never saw the books, the tablecloth, or the man again.

Exciting Moments

Callemin and Garnier want to see me, I'm told one day.

"We meet this evening at 6:30 on Rue du Temple."

I hesitated. I feared for them. But I love emotion. I went. They're both there, standing on a street corner. There was great hustle and bustle, the workshops and stores emptying out. Around them a compact, busy mass of employees and workers hastily returning home. The two fugitives seemed to be drowning in a human sea.

"Hello," Callemin said.

"Nice of you to come," Garnier added.

And we started to chat. We were blocking the traffic.

"Move along," a policeman said.

At the sight of the uniform, Callemin and Garnier in unison stuck their hands in their pockets. I shivered.

"Can't you see that you're blocking the way?" the policeman told us.

"Fine, fine … We'll move," Garnier grumbled.

We went into a nearby greasy spoon.

"Dinner is on me," said Garnier, who was always the least miserly of the bunch.

We sat at a table in the middle of the restaurant, the only one available, clearly visible. Around us the customers were eating, their heads bent over a newspaper leaning on a glass or bottle.

"One hundred thousand francs are promised to whoever turns over the bandits."

---

18 "God loves odd numbers," which supposedly bring luck. —ed.

"Quite a sum of money," a young woman sitting next to us said to her friend sitting across from her.

"Hey, a Belgian," Callemin exclaimed, recognizing his country's accent.

Turning to his neighbor, smiling like a child and exaggerating his accent, he said:

"You know, mademoiselle, you just said something really good. I've often thought the same as you. I, too, would like to benefit from these 100,000 francs. But honestly, I don't think I'll ever have that good fortune."

Garnier laughed heartily.

As for me, I swallowed with difficulty. I was a little nervous. Garnier and Callemin have become fatalist. They no longer hid, no longer taking the trouble. They march ahead, nose in the air, trusting in their lucky stars.

"They don't dare arrest us," Garnier asserted, "and this can go on for some time."

"It'll last as long as we do," Callemin concluded.

"Obviously," Kibalchich would have said.

I received a visit from Metge. He had the same pitiful look. He had a way of saying "What a mess, what a mess" that could break your heart.

I invited him to lunch. He did nothing but complain. Soudy, feeling bad for him, shared his modest fortune with him: six francs.

"Thanks," said Metge.

And as he was leaving, we could still hear him saying on the staircase, "What a mess, What a mess."

My little Chinette was beginning to know Mr. Jouin. The first time the deputy chief of the criminal brigade had arrested my husband, Louis Maîtrejean. Chinette witnessed this. Taken in by some devoted friends who lived in the suburbs, one evening my little girl saw agents of the criminal police, again led by Mr. Jouin, enter the home of her adoptive parents. Jouin left, taking with him the master of the house, who Chinettte called "Papa André."

When, preceded by a number of sleuths, Mr. Jouin entered our apartment on Rue Fessart, Chinette, seated on a tall chair, her legs dangling, gazed at him at length.

She looked pensive. She swung her legs back and forth. One of her feet banged into the knee of the deputy chief. Chinette abruptly pulled her foot back, which Mr. Jouin noticed.

"Don't worry, my little one," he gently told her. "I'm not a bad man. I won't hurt you. Don't you recognize me?"

"Of course, I recognize you perfectly," Chinette answered with her lisping voice.

Breaking out in sobs she added: "You already took away Papa Louis, then you took away Papa André, and today I'm sure you're going to take away Papa Victor."

From his expression it was clear Mr. Jouin was moved.

"Poor kid," he said.

Which didn't prevent him from taking away Kibalchich.

I found a summons under my door. Mr. Gilbert, the examining magistrate, asking me to go to his office for the fourth time. A brief visit. I tried to be witty. I slept that night at Saint-Lazare.

At Saint-Lazare Prison

I entered it poor. If anarchy doesn't feed its men, it feeds its women even less.

I'm sent to work at the workshop. There were fifty of us there. I viewed it as a kind of paradise. Which proves, yet again, that happiness is always a relative thing.

After ten days, nonanarchist friends finally took an interest in me.

There I was in the "pistole." The "pistole" is a large room whose walls are painted three-quarters black, the other quarter whitewashed. It gave the room a mournful air. Joists stuck out from the ceiling. Between each of them, spiders spun their webs undisturbed. No one thought of disturbing them. Later, when I told Kibalchich of their presence, he envied me them, so horrible was the "administrative property" of his cell.

In the middle, a tiny, rusty stove. Lined up against the wall, small cots. A bedstead, a straw mattress, two beds, a small table that each "guest" decorated as she wished. The right to the "pistole" cost four sous a day in summer, five in winter. The price didn't include wood, coal, or candles.

Above each bed ran a small plank resembling those soldiers use to pile up their kits, where we placed our clothes and linens. Six chairs, as many beds. Loose, pitted red tile floors. Greasy, thick, age-old dust clogged the interstices. The place wasn't a joyful one, but all in all it was a thousand times better than the workshop.

When I arrived, my companions questioned me. Clearly my case interested them.

"It's rare to find an anarchist in the 'pistole,'" an old habituée who was visiting told me.

A talkative woman, she declared: "During my stays here I've more often met society ladies who'd stolen a corset or a skirt in a department store, or bourgeois women who'd committed a crime of passion and prisoners from famous cases. But most of the clientele," she added, "are honest tenants like myself, who the police—whatever might be said—don't always show great tolerance for."

And thinking she'd astonish me, she threw in my face; "I met Mme. Steinheil here.[19] What a charming woman."

A Few Character Sketches

But there aren't only prisoners at Saint-Lazare; there are also "sisters."

Even if it makes most anarchist friends scream, I've preserved the tenderest, kindest, most comforting memories of them. During the year I spent at Saint-Lazare they were never anything but kindness itself toward me. Knowing my taste for dead flowers, they delicately brought me faded flowers from the Chapel of the Virgin Mary, with which I decorated my table and ornamented my walls.

Sister Léonide seemed to be a horror. She spoke loudly, her gestures choppy. She was the one who was called whenever order was seriously disturbed, which sometimes occurred.

She would arrive, her wimple flapping, her eyes aflame, and believe you me, she said precisely what she wanted to say. When

19 Marguerite Steinheil (1869–1954), the woman with whom French president Faure was having sex at the moment he died in 1899. In 1908 she would be suspected of the murder of her mother and her husband. —ed.

she arrived, fear struck the hearts of even the boldest. No one thought to stand up to her. Once calm was restored she would leave the room walking backward, like a lion tamer leaving a cage.

But one day when she hadn't closed the door quickly enough I saw her face lit up with a kind, bright smile. Good sister Léonide!

And there was the good sister Rat Catcher. That's the nickname we gave the sister who saw to the community's henhouse. This sister had maintained the heavy, determined step of the countryside from which she came. She raised hens and chicks, rabbits, ducks, and pigeons with a farmer's love.

Sometimes rats—with which Saint-Lazare was infested—ate the little broods, at which a fierce, ferocious hatred rose in that simple heart. Accompanied by a rat-catching dog, every day she frenziedly, angrily hunted rodents. How many times did I see her laying on her belly, her wimple askew, armed with a broomstick digging around in a lead pipe.

"I've got one," she exclaimed. "He's hidden away in there, the bastard."

At the end of the drainpipe the dog waited, ready to leap on the rat, who was being pushed toward him. At night, sister Rat Catcher, equipped with a lamp, carried on the hunt.

One day the chaplain was told there was an intellectual in the "pistole." He paid me a visit one Sunday afternoon. He was a tall, handsome old man, filled with kindness.

"Idle hands are the devil's plaything. Would you like to work, my child? Would you like to learn Latin?"

I didn't dare refuse him.

Chinette's Visit

My little daughter Chinette came to see me, brought by a friend. Her face took on a pained expression at the sight of the visiting room. She wouldn't speak. An elderly guard, a good, kind man, stepped forward to caress her. He offered her his hand.

"Say 'hello' to me, little one."

"No," Chinette shook her head.

"You're wrong," I said to my daughter. The gentleman doesn't want to do me any harm. He's not a wicked man."

And speaking to her in the language she understood best:
"Look at him. He's not a cop."
"If he's not wicked, let him remove the grill. After I'll kiss him."
I'm going to leave Saint-Lazare.
The date of the trial approaches.

Well-Guarded

We were transported to prison. The large "pistole" made way for a tiny cell. There, too, were sisters, good and devoted, but we were almost never under their guard. Their gentle discipline was replaced by the iron rule of the guards: we were held under the harshest of regimes. Morning and evening we were frisked, our laces and belts were taken from us, they took my pins from me. It became difficult to dress.

The same harsh rules were applied to all of the accused.

During the night the electric bulb suspended from the ceiling remained lit, casting a harsh light on the cell's white walls. It was nearly impossible to sleep. Every three minutes the little peephole in the door opened and closed.

This bothersome, close surveillance continued throughout the twenty-three days of the trial.

I was closely guarded. It made me think of the *Mona Lisa*.

During the breaks in the trial, the intermissions, as Soudy called them, we were held in two separate rooms. I was with Callemin, Soudy, Metge, de Boë,[20] Gauzy,[21] and Simentoff.[22] Kibalchich was in the other room. Gauzy never stopped moaning, getting on Callemin's nerves in the worst way.

"Don't cry, old man. You'll soon be selling leg chains," he finally said to him.

---

20 Jean de Boë (1889–1974), Belgian anarchist found guilty of complicity with the Bonnot Gang and sentenced to Devil's Island. —ed.

21 Antoine Gauzy (1879–1963), found guilty of having hidden Bonnot when the police searched for him at Gauzy's welding shop. —ed.

22 Alias of Etienne Monier (1889–1913), member of the Bonnot Gang executed on April 21, 1913. —ed.

The merchant from Ivry was painful to look at. He was desolation personified. He cried virtually nonstop for twenty-three days. He held out his hands to his guards. They, thinking he was asking to go out, put handcuffs on him. Those were the orders.

That was what we had to have on even to go to a certain place. In order to obtain a little more discretion, I had to ask an officer to intervene.

Metge becomes Mystical

Metge revealed himself in an unexpected light. He became mystical. The beyond worried him.

"All I ask," he confided in us, "is not to be sentenced to death."

And in response to Soudy's mocking look: "It's not that I'm afraid of the guillotine," he quickly added. "No, if I have to go there I'll go there proudly. But you have to admit that it's a real pain not to know what goes on in the other life, while if I was only sentenced to forced labor I could organize another life for myself. I love the country."

At which he imagined a happy life, already seeing a little farm, a farmyard full of animals. He even saw his farmer wife. In certain books the penal colony seems like a resort. Metge hadn't read much, but he had read that. Don't try to demonstrate that it was the opposite; you'd be wasting your time. Carouy listened and smiled.

Callemin was the same as ever, pronouncing sermons.

"You were really lower than low," he said to one.

"You never should have said that," he told another.

Everyone was subject to his criticism.

While at Santé Prison Metge and Soudy had found a way to communicate. How they did so is their secret. Soudy had written poetry he'd sent to his fellow prisoner. Metge found it admirable. Soudy a poet, Metge a critic: all this was beyond me. Soudy had confided in me: "It's not as tough as all that to write verses. All they have to do is rhyme."

"And the feet?"

"What feet?"

The Man with the Rifle

Every time he glimpsed me Soudy made a face. That was his way of saying "hello." The guard who accompanied him noticed this.

"No mistake about it," the guard said. "You're the man with the rifle. All the witnesses who saw what happened on the square in Chantilly agree that the individual who fired grimaced."

"Nothing but a coincidence," said Soudy.

Soudy loved talking with his guards, attempting to persuade them. His favorite theme was all forms of crookedness. It was the only subject he knew thoroughly, and he could speak for hours about it.

There are several sorts of crooked schemes. There's the little one, which begins with the swiping of a tin of sardines and ends with a dozen of them: this is where you begin. Then there's theft pure and simple. This should ensure you a more comfortable existence. It also requires more experience. First you have to learn how to jimmy a door open. Sometimes the door is only a simple drawer. It's good to start small …

"Nothing's easier," Soudy assured us.

"?"

"You want me to show you how to go about it?" and he advanced to the door.

"Halt!" the guards said. "We already know how to open that door."

Callemin the Misogynist

Of all the things Callemin hated, his hatred of women was the greatest. At least, that's what he said. In Brussels he'd been the platonic lover of a young Russian woman, and he sincerely hoped never again to go through that experience, even in more complete a form. He'd sworn this to himself.

These kinds of vows are rarely kept.

After Rue Ordener, Raymond-la-Science began to make exceptions to his principles. He made even greater ones after the Chantilly Affair. He ran into a woman. He knew her quite well. She was kind, welcoming, excused everything. Even more, she glorified everything. Callemin, charmed, was won over.

From concession to concession—once you're on that slippery slope you never know when to stop—he agreed to accompany her to hear some music. This, too, was against all his former principles. The two lovers attended all the classical concerts. Every evening, arm in arm, they strolled up Rue de la Tour-d'Auvergne. Dreams of their future were outlined. At Porte de Jourdan, where Callemin lived, they went their separate ways.

One evening they were followed. Raymond, ever on the alert, immediately noticed it.

"That man bothers me," he said.

"Don't worry," the woman answered. "He's nothing but someone walking behind us."

"Or a policeman."

"No, he's too well dressed."

Callemin relaxed. The next day he was arrested. At first he was knocked for a loop. Taken to the police station, having regained his composure, there was one man in particular who attracted his attention.

I saw that face somewhere, he said to himself over and over again. Suddenly, it hit him.

"I've got it! It's the man who was walking behind me yesterday. What's his name?"

"That's Mr. Jouin," a policeman answered.

"Isn't that amazing," Callemin said to me during a break in the trial. "And yet, *she* is above suspicion," he added with certainty.

Verses

Soudy recited some verses directed to me:

> Rirette, do you remember
> The Buttes-Chaumont?
> The sunny park? The suspended bridge?
> The lake, a bit deep
> And the temple of Love
> From which the lovers
> Escaped from the factories

>Return entwined
>To pass over the red brick bridge?

Metge was in a state of rapture, already seeing his pastoral dream before him.

"Not bad," said a guard, nodding his head knowingly.

I was deeply touched. I thought of the time not so long ago when Soudy would take my two little girls, Maud and Chinette, to the peaceful garden of swarming Belleville.

How much had happened since.

It was all in the past. The future remained.

In the final days of the trial Callemin again became sentimental and lyrical. He would sometimes sigh. What was he thinking of? Perhaps of his first and final adventures, which for him would end so badly. He confided to me: "I'd gladly agree to no longer be scientific." And he added between clenched teeth: "For a woman. It's sad at my age to be reduced to marrying 'the widow.'"[23]

I did my thinking in my cell. The place of honor I was given among the defendants worried me some. I constantly heard talk of an organized gang. But as I knew, if there was anything that was missing in this gang it was organization.

"We always proceeded blindly," Callemin told me. "We left for one job and committed another. The one on Rue Ordener was off the cuff. The morning of Chantilly we still didn't know where we were going. We lacked a head."

Bourgeois reason no differently, and this frightens me.

If they see me as the head then I'm done for.

The Shortcomings of Science

Only once in my life did I hear Callemin admit to his inferiority.

I was seated first in the front row of the defendants. Raymond-la-Science, first in the second row, was seated directly behind me. What my questioning was like I barely remember.

The first one questioned, I was quite embarrassed. I seemed to be boasting, I've been told, but in fact I've never in my life been

---

23 Slang for the guillotine. —ed.

so nervous. There was a kind of fog before my eyes that prevented me from seeing the courtroom and making out the members of the jury. My voice seemed to come from afar, choked, strange. It was unspeakably difficult to swallow my saliva.

"You may be seated," the presiding judge said to me.

I collapsed onto the bench, my forehead damp, my mind empty. I felt breathing on my neck, a voice whispering in my ear, those of Callemin: "You were good, really good."

The next day it was Raymond-la-Science's turn. He got tangled up in his sentences, his statements unclear, and finally came up empty-handed. When he finished, I turned toward him, he leaned toward me and, disconsolate, saddened, his voice low, he said, "That was pretty weak, eh?"

Which didn't prevent him the next day from insulting the others during the breaks in the trial.

The Great Fear in Criminal Court

Throughout the trial I only had eyes for the prosecutor, Fabre. His red robe invariably attracted my gaze. He wore it with a sober and cold elegance. When he entered along with the judges I unreservedly admired the majesty of his step. One could feel his awareness of the terrible role he fulfilled as the one to mete out justice . For twenty-three days he would follow, without tiring, without a flaw, these long, mortal debates. I kept an eye on him. Not a single detail escaped him. I had the clear impression that he sought the truth with a frightful fierceness. When he finally rose for his final summation, an icy cold passed through my bones.

A clear, cutting, severe voice rose in the silence of the courtroom. Hearing him, I understood that "society" crushed all who do not want to accept its laws. I was conscious of having before me an unheard of, prodigious force against which it was impossible for the pitiful theories of illegalism to prevail. I was witnessing a terrible lesson. At the end of certain phrases, I could hear in my wobbling brain the dry sound of a blade. That terrifying man!

When the prosecutor took his seat, amid the general emotion I fearfully, involuntarily glanced at several of my companions. They understood the look in my eye.

And their entire attitude seemed to respond: "We're done for."

February 25—Evening

We have finally reached the end. Only the last defense speech left to hear. Tomorrow the verdict.

We're exhausted. The cheekiness and bravado some of us have adopted are for show. Deep down we are all mortally worried. Attorney Adad again gave me encouragement. For the past few days I've been relegated to the third bench.

"Don't worry," he tells me. "When the verdict is read you'll assume your place in the first row in the first seat."

I receive a hammer blow. I can no longer fool myself: I get the maximum, twenty years. Here we are in our common room. One last time Callemin wants to show off. He tells the guards, "I'll die when I'm good and ready."

The result: we're frisked more seriously than usual, the least fold in our clothing scrutinized. The smallest hem of my smock is unstitched. The linings of our clothes are gone over with a fine-tooth comb. And on some of us the liberating drug is found.

On the twenty-sixth, at 11:45, we enter the courtroom. Kibalchich is calm and smiling. The previous day he'd written me: "My friend, I ask for the both of our sakes that you resign yourself in advance to the worst solution. Don't forget that I can only be strong if you are with me and for me. At bottom, my friend, what difference is our lot if we can help each other vanquish it and if we know that whatever might happen we will meet again one day."[24]

Kibalchich and I had since the beginning renounced the "tu" form when addressing each other, fed up as we were of also being addressed familiarly by all those around us.

The final defense plea. The presiding judge questioned us one last time. A few final declamations. Reading of the questions. How many formalities! The jury finally withdrew.

After a wait of half an hour in the defendants' room it's decided to return us to our cells. It's 3:00. We're given the order to eat quickly. A visit from our attorney Adad.

---

24 All of this was expressed using the formal "vous" form. —ed.

"The verdict will be delivered round nine in the evening," he tells me.

I eat some soup. I drink some milk and begin to pace my cell like a caged animal. I try to read. Impossible. The lines dance before my eyes. Nuns come to see me. The mother superior of the prison brings me hot tea mixed with rum. I think of the others. Of those who, like me, are pacing in their cells.

At 8:00 I'm told that the jury members are discussing the hundred and fiftieth question. There are four hundred. "Well there you go," Soudy says. My nerves on edge, I lay down fully dressed on my cot. Resting under such conditions is impossible. I resume my stroll around my little room.

11:00 P.M.

"Come," the guard says.

Frisked again. This time everything is forbidden. A chocolate bar, a tiny mirror, a small pencil, a blank piece of paper that they were kind enough to allow me to keep after the last time I was frisked, are now confiscated. I'm left only my handkerchief. They foresee that I'm going to cry. Our steps echo loudly in the corridors of the sleeping prison. We're again led into the small defendants' room.

I gave a start upon entering. The fifty municipal police assigned to guard us had eaten and drunk there. The floor is covered in egg shells, in bread crusts, in greasy papers. They've also smoked there, as the many cigarette butts spread across the floor attest. The odor of pipe tobacco and cheap wine float in the air. A violent odor of garlic completes the picture.

"Open the window," I begged.

"Impossible," the guards respond. "It's forbidden."

"At least sweep up the mess."

"Also forbidden."

The officer on duty, who throughout those long days was always exquisitely polite, expressed his regrets. His men had formal orders to not let us out of their sight for a second and not to allow us the least unexpected gesture. Mr. Desmoulins comes to visit us amid the stench. He brings us chocolate and some sweets. The guards are nervous, worried.

We remained there, shut in, cooped up, piled in from 11:00 at night till 5:00 the next morning.

An odd nervousness gripped Callemin, de Boë, and me. We started speaking loudly, very loudly. The sound of our voices reached the neighboring room, where Kibalchich was being held. He came up to the door separating us. He looked at me with curiosity. Soudy joined in, making use of his entire stock of slang. We spoke so loudly and for so long about things having nothing to do with the trial that a guard went to find the officer on duty, who listened to us for fifteen minutes. He gave an astonished smile and left, feeling for us.

Suddenly, a name loudly resounded: "Madame Maîtrejean."

I felt a shock. It's finally over! I hurried, running to the door, blowing a kiss to Kibalchich. I wave to the rest and pass quickly, quickly. I'm in a hurry to know.

In the corridor next to the courtroom the guards are gathered together, commanded by two officers. Rodriguez, the Vuillemain woman, and little Barbe Leclerc arrive. And the port brutally closes.

I understand. We're the only ones acquitted.

A sob, a shout: "And Kibalchich!"

One of the officers comes over to me.

"Don't cry, madame. Kibalchich will receive a short sentence, six months, perhaps a year, very little. He'll be free at the same time as you. Don't cry . . ."[25]

The door giving onto the courtroom opens. I glimpse a sinister gray light. I hear the monotone voice of the judge. I'm told to rise. I'm told to sit. They shout at me: "Answer yes ... Answer no ... express your thanks."

I later learned the room was filled to bursting. We're told to leave. We never saw the others again, not even for a second.

---

25 In fact, Kibalchich/Serge received a five-year sentence, which he served in full. He was expelled from France upon his release and went to Spain, where he became active in anarcho-syndicalist circles. Victor and Rirette married while he was in prison so she could have increased visitation rights, but their relationship effectively ended there. —ed.

In a friendly house where I took refuge that evening, I received a pneumatic letter from Kibalchich:

"My friend, I am happy you've been freed and that I am the only one suffering. Everything will come to an end. Make sure Chinette maintains her affection for me. Take advantage of the sun, the flowers, of good books, of everything we love together. But I ask of you from the bottom of my heart, never return to that milieu."

Where has it gone, the time when, convinced, my friend asserted: "There are things to be done, there's something to be done."

This time the experience was decisive.

No, I will not return to that "milieu." You can rest easy. I swear it, my friend.

AK Press is small, in terms of staff and resources, but we also manage to be one of the world's most productive anarchist publishing houses. We publish close to twenty books every year, and distribute thousands of other titles published by like-minded independent presses and projects from around the globe. We're entirely worker-run and democratically managed. We operate without a corporate structure—no boss, no managers, no bullshit.

The FRIENDS OF AK program is a way you can directly contribute to the continued existence of AK PRESS, and ensure that we're able to keep publishing books like this one! FRIENDS pay $25 a month directly into our publishing account ($30 for Canada, $35 for international), and receive a copy of every book AK PRESS publishes for the duration of their membership! Friends also receive a discount on anything they order from our website or buy at a table: 50% on AK titles, and 20% on everything else. We have a FRIENDS OF AK ebook program as well: $15 a month gets you an electronic copy of every book we publish for the duration of your membership. You can even sponsor a very discounted membership for someone in prison.

Email friendsofak@akpress.org for more info, or visit the FRIENDS OF AK PRESS website: https://www.akpress.org/friends.html.

There are always great book projects in the works—so sign up now to become a FRIEND OF AK PRESS, and let the presses roll!